ON

THE STUDY OF WORDS

BY

RICHARD CHENEVIX TRENCH, B.D.,

VICAR OF ITCHENSTOKE, HANTS; EXAMINING CHAPLAIN TO THE LORD BISHOP OF OXFORD; AND PROFESSOR OF DIVINITY, KING'S COLLEGE, LONDON.

FROM THE SECOND LONDON EDITION, REVISED AND ENLARGED.

REDFIELD,

110 AND 112 NASSAU STREET, NEW YORK.

[Ninth Edition.] 1855.

PREFACE

TO

THE FIRST EDITION.

THESE lectures will not, I trust, be found anywhere to have left out of sight seriously, or for long, the peculiar needs of those for whom they were originally intended, and to whom they were primarily addressed. I am conscious indeed, here and there, of a certain departure from my first intention, having been in part seduced to this by a circumstance which I had not in the least contemplated when I obtained permission to deliver them, by finding, namely, that I should have other hearers besides the pupils of the training school. Some matter adapted for those rather than for these I was thus led to introduce—which afterward I was unwilling in preparing for the press, to remove; on the contrary adding to it rather, in the hope of obtaining thus a somewhat wider circle of readers than I could have hoped, had I more rigidly restricted myself in the choice of my materials. Yet I should greatly regret to have admitted so much of this as should deprive these lectures of their fitness for those whose profit in writing and in publishing I had mainly in view, namely, schoolmasters and those preparing to be such.

Had I known any book entering with any fullness, and in a popular manner, into the subject-matter of these pages, and making it its exclusive theme, I might still have delivered these lectures, but should scarcely have sought for them a wider audience than their first, gladly leaving the matter in their hands, whose studies in language had been fuller and riper than my own. But abundant and ready to hand, as are the materials for such a book, I did not; while yet it seems to me that the subject is one to which it is beyond measure desirable that their attention, who are teaching, or shall have hereafter to teach, others should be directed; so that they shall learn to regard language as one of the chiefest organs of their own education and that of others. For I am persuaded that I have used no exaggeration in saying, that for many a young man "his first discovery that words are living powers, has been like the dropping of scales from his eyes, like the acquiring of another sense, or the introduction into a new world,"—while yet all this may be indefinitely deferred, may, indeed, never find place at all, unless there is some one at hand to help for him and to hasten the process; and he who so does, will ever after be esteemed by him as one of his very foremost benefactors. Whatever may be Horne Tooke's shortcomings, whether in occasional details of etymology, or in the philosophy of grammar, or in matters more serious still, yet, with all this, what an epoch in many a student's intellectual life has been his first acquaintance with *The Diversions of Purley*. And they were not among the least of the obligations of the young men of our time to Coleridge, that he so often himself weighed words in the balances, and so earnestly pressed upon all with whom his voice went for anything, the profit which they would find in so doing. Nor, with the certainty that I am inticipating much in my little volume, can I refrain from quoting some words which were not present with me during its composition, although I must have been familiar with them long ago, words which express excellently well why it is that these studies profit so much, and which will also explain the motives which induced me to add my little contribution to their furtherance:—

"A language will often be wiser, not merely than the vulgar, but even than the wisest of those who speak it. Being like amber in its efficacy to circulate the electric spirit of truth, it is also like amber in embalming and preserving the relics of ancient wisdom, although one is not seldom puzzled to decipher its contents. Sometimes it locks up truths, which were once well known, but which, in the course of ages, have passed out of sight and been forgotten. In other cases it holds the germs of truths, of which, though they were never plainly discerned, the genius of its framers caught a glimpse in a happy moment of divination. A meditative man can not refrain from wonder, when he digs down to the deep thought lying at the root of many a metaphorical term, employed for the designation of spiritual things, even of those with regard to which professing philosophers have blundered grossly; and often it would seem as though rays of truths, which were still below the intellectual horizon, had dawned upon the imagination as it was looking up to heaven. Hence they who feel an inward call to teach and enlighten their countrymen, should deem it an important part of their duty to draw out the stores of thought which are al ready latent in their native language, to purify it from the corruptions which time brings upon all things, and from which language has no exemption, and to endeavor to give distinctness and precision to whatever in it is confused, or obscure, or dimly seen."*

I will only add, that if I have not owned one by one my obligations to each writer who has helped me here—obligations which readers familiar with the subject will recognise at once—this has arisen from no desire to escape the acknowledgment, but only from the popular character of these lectures, in which multiplied references would have been plainly out of place.

ITCHENSTOKE, *Oct.* 9, 1851.

* *Guesses at Truth*, First Series, p. 295.

PREFACE TO THE SECOND EDITION.

I HAVE availed myself of the opportunities which a second edition has afforded me, for the correcting of some few errors in the first, which either I had myself discovered, or which publicly or privately had been pointed out to me. I have also added a sixth lecture to the five which at first composed this series; and by other additions, as once or twice by omission, have sought to render this little volume less unworthy of the favor which it has found.

ITCHENSTOKE, *Feb.* 4, 1852.

ON

THE STUDY OF WORDS.

INTRODUCTORY LECTURE.

There are few who would not readily acknowledge that in worthy books is laid up and hoarded the greater part of the treasures of wisdom and knowledge which the world has accumulated; and that chiefly by aid of these they are handed down from one generation to another. My purpose in the present, and in some succeeding lectures, which by the kindness of your principal, I shall have the opportunity of addressing to you here, is to urge on you something different from this; namely, that not in books only, which all acknowledge, nor yet in connected oral discourse, but often also in words contemplated singly, there are boundless stores of moral and historic truth, and no less of passion and imagination, laid up—lessons of infinite worth which we may derive from them, if only our attention is awakened to their existence. I would urge on you, though with teaching such as you enjoy, the subject will not be new to you, how well it will repay you to study the words which you are in the habit of using or of meeting, be they such as relate to highest spiritual things, or our common words of the shop and the market, and all the familiar intercourse of life. It will indeed repay you far better than you can easily believe. I am sure, at least, that for many a young man his first discovery of the fact that words are living powers, has been like the dropping of scales from his eyes, like the acquiring of another sense, or the introduction into a new world; he is never able to cease wondering at the moral marvels that surround him on every side, and ever reveal themselves more and more to his gaze.

We indeed hear it not seldom said that ignorance is the mother of admiration. A falser word was never spoken, and hardly a more mischievous one; for it seems to imply that this healthiest exercise of the mind rests, for the most part, on a deceit and illusion and that with better knowledge it would cease. For once that ignorance leads us to admire that which with fuller insight we should perceive to be a common thing, and one demanding therefore no such tribute from us, a hundred, nay, a thousand times, it prevents us from admiring that which is admirable indeed. This is true, whether we are moving in the region of nature, which is the region of God's wonders, or even in the region of art, which is the region of man's wonders; and nowhere truer than in this sphere and region of language, which is about to claim us now. Oftentimes here we move up and down in the midst of intellectual and moral marvels with vacant eye and with careless mind, even as some traveller passes unmoved over fields of fame, or through cities of ancient renown — unmoved because utterly unconscious of the great deeds which there have been wrought, of the great hearts which spent themselves there. We, like him, wanting the knowledge and insight which would have served to kindle admiration in us, are oftentimes deprived of this pure and elevating excitement of the mind, and miss no less that manifold teaching and instruction which ever lie about our path, and nowhere more largely than in our daily words, if only we knew how to put forth our hands and make it our own. "What riches," one exclaims, "lie hidden in the vulgar tongue of our poorest and most ignorant. What flowers of paradise lie under our feet, with their beauties and their parts undistinguished and undiscerned, from having been daily trodden on."

And this subject upon which we are thus entering ought not to be a dull or uninteresting one in the handling, or one to which only by an effort you will yield the attention which I shall claim. If it shall prove so, this I fear must be through the fault of my manner of treating it; for certainly in itself there is no study which *may* be made at once more instructive and entertaining than the study of the use, origin, and distinction of words, which is exactly that which I now propose to myself and to you. I remember a very learned scholar, to whom we owe one of our best Greek lexicons, a book which must have cost him years, speaking in the preface to his great work with a just disdain of some, who complained of the irksome drudgery of such toils as those which had engaged him so long—and this, forsooth, because they only had to do with words; who claimed pity for themselves, as though they had been so many galley-slaves chained to the oar, or martyrs who had offered themselves to the good of the rest of the literary world. He declares that, for his part, the task of classing, sorting, grouping, comparing, tracing the derivation and usage of words, had been to him no drudgery, but a delight and labor of love.

And if this may be true in regard of a foreign tongue, how much truer ought it to be in regard of our own, of our "mother-tongue," as we fondly call it. A great writer not very long departed from us has here borne witness at once to the pleasantness and profit of this study. "In a language," he says, "like ours, where so many words are derived from other languages, there are few modes of instruction more useful or more amusing than that of accustoming young people to seek for the etymology or primary meaning of the words they use. There are cases in which more knowledge of more value may be conveyed by the history of a word than by the history of a campaign."

And, implying the same truth, a popular American author has somewhere characterized language as "fossil poetry"—evidently meaning that just as in some fossil, curious and beautiful shapes of vegetable or animal life, the graceful fern or the finely vertebrated lizard, such as now, it may be, have been extinct for thousands of years, are permanently bound up with the stone, and rescued from that perishing which would have otherwise been theirs—so in words are beautiful thoughts and images, the imagination and the feeling of past ages, of men long since in their graves, of men whose very names have perished, these, which would so easily have perished too, preserved and made safe for ever. The phrase is a striking one; the only fault which one might be tempted to find with it is, that it is too narrow. Language may be, and indeed is, this "fossil poetry;" but it may be affirmed of it with exactly the same truth that it is fossil ethics, or fossil history. Words quite as often and as effectually embody facts of history, or convictions of the moral common sense, as of the imagination or passion of men; even as, so far as that moral sense may be perverted, they will bear witness and keep a record of that perversion. On all these points I shall enter at full in after lectures; but I may give by anticipation a specimen or two of what I mean to make from the first my purpose and plan more fully intelligible to all.

Language, then, is fossil poetry; in other words, we are not to look for the poetry which a people may possess only in its poems, or its poetical customs, traditions, and beliefs. Many a single word also is itself a concentrated poem, having stores of poetical thought and imagery laid up in it. Examine it, and it will be found to rest on some deep analogy of things natural and things spiritual; bringing those to illustrate and to give an abiding form and body to these. The image may have grown trite and ordinary now; perhaps through the help of this very word may have become so entirely the heritage of all, as to seem little better than a commonplace; yet not the less he who first discerned the relation, and devised the new word which should express it, or gave to an old, never before but literally used, this new and figurative sense, this man was in his degree a poet—a maker, that is, of things which were not before, which would not have existed, but for him, or for some other gifted with equal powers.

He who spake first of a "dilapidated" fortune, what an image must have risen up before his mind's eye of some falling house or palace, stone detaching itself from stone, till all had gradually sunk into desolation and ruin. Or he who to that Greek word which signifies "that which will endure to be held up to and judged by the sunlight," gave first its ethical signification of "sincere," "truthful," or as we sometimes say, "transparent," can we deny to him the poet's feeling and eye? Many a man had gazed, we may be sure, at the jagged and indented mountain ridges of Spain, before one called them "sierras" or "saws," the name by which now they are known, as Sierra Morena, Sierra Nevada; but that man coined his imagination into a word, which will endure as long as the everlasting hills which he named.

"Iliads without a Homer," some one has called, with a little exaggeration, the beautiful but anonymous ballad poetry of Spain. One may be permitted, perhaps, to push the exaggeration a little further in the same direction, and to apply the phrase not merely to a ballad but to a word. Let me illustrate that which I have been here saying somewhat more at length by the word "tribulation." We all know in a general way that this word, which occurs not seldom in scripture and in the liturgy, means affliction, sorrow, anguish; but it is quite worth our while to know *how* it means this, and to question the word a little closer. It is derived from the Latin "tribulum"—which was the thrashing instrument or roller, whereby the Roman husbandman separated the corn from the husks; and "tribulatio" in its primary significance was the act of this separation. But some Latin writer of the Christian church appropriated the word and image for the setting forth of a higher truth; and sorrow, distress, and adversity, being the appointed means for the separating in men of their chaff from their wheat, of whatever in them was light and trivial and poor from the solid and the true, therefore he called these sorrows and griefs "tribulations," thrashings, that is, of the inner spiritual man, without which there could be no fitting him for the heavenly garner. Now in proof of what I have just now said, namely that a single word is often a concentrated poem, a little grain of gold capable of being beaten out into a broad extent of gold-leaf, I will quote, in reference to this very word "tribulation," a graceful composition by an early English poet, which you will at once perceive is all wrapped up in this word, being from first to last only the expanding of the image and thought which this word has implicitly given:—

"Till from the straw, the flail, the corn doth beat,
Until the chaff be purgéd from the wheat,
Yea, till the mill the grains in pieces tear,
The richness of the flour will scarce appear.
So, till men's persons great afflictions touch,
If worth be found, their worth is not so much,
Because, like wheat in straw, they have not yet
That value which in thrashing they may get.
For till the bruising flails of God's corrections
Have thrashéd out of us our vain affections;
Till those corruptions which do misbecome us
Are by thy sacred Spirit winnowed from us;

Until from us the straw of worldly treasures,
Till all the dusty chaff of empty pleasures,
Yea, till His flail upon us He doth lay,
To thrash the husk of this our flesh away;
And leave the soul uncovered; nay yet more,
Till God shall make our very spirit poor,
We shall not up to highest wealth aspire;
But then we shall; and that is my desire."

This deeper religious use of the word "tribulation" was unknown to classical, that is to heathen antiquity, and belongs exclusively to the Christian writers: and the fact that the same deepening and elevating of the use of words recurs in a multitude of other, and many of them far more striking instances, is one well deserving to be followed up. Nothing, I think, would more strongly bring before us what a new power Christianity was in the world than to compare the meaning which so many words possessed before its rise, and the deeper meaning which they obtained, so soon as they were assumed by it as the vehicles of its life, the new thought and feeling enlarging, purifying, and ennobling the very words which they employed. This is a subject which I shall have occasion to touch on more than once in these lectures, but is itself well worthy of, as it would afford ample material for, a volume.

But it was said just now that words often contain a witness for great moral truths—God having impressed such a seal of truth upon language, that men are continually uttering deeper things than they know, asserting mighty principles, it may be asserting them against themselves, in words that to them may seem nothing more than the current coin of society. Thus to what grand moral purposes Bishop Butler turns the word "pastime;" how seldom is the testimony which he compels the world, out of its own use of this word, to render against itself—obliging it to own that its amusements and pleasures do not really satisfy the mind and fill it as with the sense of abiding and satisfying joy;* they are only "pastime;" they serve only, as this word confesses, to *pass* away the *time*, to prevent it from weighing an intolerable burden on men's hands; all which they can do at the best is to prevent men from discovering and attending to their own internal poverty and dissatisfaction and want. He might have added that there is the same acknowledgment in the word "diversion," which means no more that that which *diverts* or turns us aside from ourselves, and in this way helps us to forget ourselves for a little. And thus it would appear that, even according to the world's own confession, all which it proposes is—not to make us happy, but a little to prevent us from remembering that we are unhappy, to *pass* away our *time*, to *divert* us from ourselves. While on the other hand we declare that the good which *will* really fill our souls and satisfy them to the uttermost, is not *in* us, but *without* us and *above* us, in the

* Sermon XIV. Upon the Love of God.

words which we use to set forth any transcending delight. Take three or four of these words—"transport," "rapture," ravishment," "ecstasy"—"transport," that which *carries* us, as "rapture," or "ravishment," that which *snatches* us, out of and above ourselves; and "ecstasy" is very nearly the same, only drawn from the Greek.

And not less, where a perversion of the moral sense has found place, words preserve oftentimes a record of this perversion. We have a signal example of this, even as it is a notable evidence of the manner in which moral contagion, spreading from heart and manners, invades the popular language in the use, or rather misuse of the word "religion," during all the ages of papal domination in Europe. Probably many of you are aware that in those times a "religious person" did not mean any one who felt and allowed the bonds that bound him to God and to his fellow-men, but one who had taken peculiar vows upon him, a member of one of the monkish orders; a "religious" house did not mean, nor does it now mean in the church of Rome a Christian household, ordered in the fear of God, but a house in which these persons were gathered together according to the rule of some man, Benedict, or Dominic or some other. A "religion" meant not a service of God, but an order of monkery; and taking the monastic vows was termed going into a "religion." Now what an awful light does this one word so used throw on the entire state of mind and habits of thought in those ages! That then was "religion," and nothing else was deserving of the name! And "religious," was a title which might not be given to parents and children, husbands and wives, men and women fulfilling faithfully and holily in the world the several duties of their stations, but only to those who had devised self-chosen service for themselves.*

In like manner that "lewd," which meant at one time no more than "lay," or unlearned — the "lewd" people, the lay people — should come to signify the sinful, the vicious, is not a little worthy of note. How forcibly we are reminded here of that saying of the Pharisees of old: "This people which knoweth not the law is cursed;" how much of their spirit must have been at work before the word could have acquired this secondary meaning.

But language is fossil history as well. What a record of great social revolutions, revolutions in nations and in the feelings of nations, the one word "frank" contains; which is used, as we all know, to

* A reviewer in *Fraser's Magazine*, December, 1851, in the main a favorable, and always a kind one, doubts whether I have not here pushed my assertion too far. So far from this being the case, it was not merely "the popular language," as I have expressed myself, which this corruption had invaded, but a decree of the great Fourth Lateran Council, forbidding the further multiplication of monastic orders, runs thus: Ne nimia *religionum* diversitas gravem in Ecclesiâ Dei confusionem inducat, firmiter prohibemus, ne quis de cetero novam *religionem* inveniat, sed quicunque voluerit ad *religionem* converti, unam de approbatis assumat.

express aught that is generous, straightforward, and free. The Franks, I need not remind you, were a powerful German tribe, or association of tribes, which at the breaking up of the Roman empire possessed themselves of Gaul, to which they gave their own name. They were the ruling conquering people, honorably distinguished from the Gauls and degenerate Romans among whom they established themselves by their independence, their love of freedom, their scorn of a lie: they had, in short, the virtues which belong to a conquering and dominant race in the midst of an inferior and conquered one. And thus it came to pass that by degrees the name "frank," which may have originally indicated merely a national, came to involve a moral distinction as well; and a "frank" man was synonymous not merely with a man of the conquering German race, but was an epithet applied to a person possessed of certain high moral qualities, which for the most part appertained to, and were found only in men of that stock; and thus in men's daily discourse, when they speak of a person as being "frank," or when they use the words "franchise," "enfranchisement," to express civil liberties and immunities, their language here is the outgrowth, the record, and the result of great historic changes, bears testimony to facts of history, whereof it may well happen that the speakers have never heard. Let me suggest to you the word "slave," as one which has undergone a process entirely analogous, although in an opposite direction.*

Having given by anticipation this handful of examples in illustration of what in these lectures I propose, I will, before proceeding further, make a few observations on a subject, which, if we would go at all to the root of the matter, we can scarcely leave altogether untouched—I mean the origin of language; in which yet we will not entangle ourselves deeper than we need. There are, or rather there have been, two theories about this. One, and that which rather has been than now is, for few maintain it still, would put language on the same level with the various arts and inventions with which man has gradually adorned and enriched his life. It would make him by degrees to have invented it, just as he might have invented any of these, for himself; and from rude imperfect beginnings, the inarticulate cries by which he expressed his natural wants, the sounds by which he sought to imitate the impression of natural objects upon him, little by little to have arrived at that wondrous organ of thought and feeling, which his language is often to him now.

It might, I think, be sufficient to object to this explanation, that language would then be an *accident* of human nature; and, this being the case, that we certainly should somewhere encounter tribes sunken

* See Gibbon's *Decline and Fall*, c. 55.

so low as not to possess it; even as there is no human art or invention, though it be as simple and obvious as the preparing of food by fire, but there are those who have fallen below its exercise. But with language it is not so. There have never yet been found human beings, not the most degraded horde of South African bushmen, or Papuan cannibals, who did not employ this means of intercourse with one another. But the more decisive objection to this view of the matter is, that it hangs together with, and is indeed an essential part of that theory of society, which is contradicted alike by every page of Genesis, and every notice of our actual experience —the "orang-outang" theory, as it has been so happily termed—that, I mean, according to which the primitive condition of man was the savage one, and the savage himself the seed out of which in due time the civilized man was unfolded; whereas, in fact, so far from being this living seed, he might more justly be considered as a dead withered leaf, torn violently away from the great trunk of humanity, and with no more power to produce anything nobler than himself out of himself, than that dead, withered leaf to unfold itself into the oak of the forest. So far from being the child with the latent capacities of manhood, he is himself rather the man prematurely aged, and decrepit, and outworn.

But the true answer to the inquiry how language arose, is this, that God gave man language, just as he gave him reason, and just because he gave him reason (for what is man's word but his reason coming forth, so that it may behold itself?) that he gave it to him, because he could not be man, that is a social being, without it. Yet this must not be taken to affirm that man started at the first furnished with a full-formed vocabulary of words, and as it were with his first dictionary and first grammar ready-made to his hands. He did not thus begin the world with names, but with the power of naming; for man is not a mere speaking machine; God did not teach him words, as one of us teaches a parrot, from without; but gave him a capacity, and then evoked the capacity which he gave. Here, as in everything else that concerns the primitive constitution, the great original institutes of humanity, our best and truest lights are to be gotten from the study of the first three chapters of Genesis; and you will observe that there it is not God who imposed the first names on the creatures, but Adam—Adam, however, at the direct suggestion of his Creator. He brought them all, we are told, to Adam, "to see what he would call them, and whatsoever Adam called every living creature, that was the name thereof." (Gen. ii. 19.) Here we have the clearest intimation of the origin, at once divine and human, of speech; while yet neither is so brought forward as to exclude or obscure the other.

And so far we may concede a limited amount of

right to those who have held a progressive acquisition, on man's part, of the power of embodying thought in words. I believe that we should conceive the actual case most truly, if we conceived this power of naming things and expressing their relations, as one laid up in the depths of man's being, one of the divine capacities with which he was created: but one (and in this differing from those which have produced in various people various arts of life), which could not remain dormant in him, for man could be only man through its exercise; which therefore did rapidly bud and blossom out from within him at every solicitation from the world without, or from his fellow-man; as each object to be named appeared before his eyes, each relation of things to one another arose before his mind. It was not the possible only, but the necessary emanation of the spirit with which he had been endowed. Man makes his own language, but he makes it as the bee makes its cells, as the bird its nest.

How this latent power evolved itself first, how this spontaneous generation of language came to pass, is a mystery, even as every act of creation is of necessity such; and as a mystery all the deepest inquirers into the subject are content to leave it. Yet we may perhaps a little help ourselves to the realizing of what the process was, and what it was not, if we liken it to the growth of a tree springing out of, and unfolding itself from a root, and according to a necessary law—that root being the divine capacity of language with which man was created, that law being the law of highest reason with which he was endowed: if we liken it to this rather than to the rearing of a house, which a man should slowly and painfully fashion for himself with dead timbers combined after his own fancy and caprice; and which little by little improved in shape, material, and size, being first but a log-house, answering his barest needs, and only after centuries of toil and pain growing for his sons' sons into a stately palace for pleasure and delight.

Were it otherwise, were the savage the primitive man, we should then find savage tribes furnished, it might be, scantily enough with the elements of speech yet at the same time with its fruitful beginnings, its vigorous and healthful germs. But what does their language on close inspection prove? In every case what they are themselves, the remnant and ruin of a better and a nobler past. Fearful indeed is the impress of degradation which is stamped on the language of the savage—more fearful perhaps even than that which is stamped upon his form. When wholly letting go the truth, when long and greatly sinning against light and conscience, a people has thus gone the downward way, has been scattered off by some violent revolution from that portion of the world which is the seat of advance and progress, and driven to its remote isles and further corners, then as one nobler thought, one spiritual idea after another has perished from it, the words also that expressed these have perished too: as a people has let go one habit of civilization after another, the words also which those habits demanded have dropped, first out of use, and then out of memory, and thus after awhile have been wholly lost.

Moffat, in his *Missionary Labors and Scenes in South Africa*, gives us a very remarkable example of the disappearing of one of the most significant words from the language of a tribe sinking ever deeper in savagery; and with the disappearing of the word of course the disappearing as well of the great spiritual fact and truth whereof that word was at once the vehicle and the guardian. The Bechuanas, a Caffre tribe, employed formerly the word "Morimo," to designate "Him that is above," or "Him that is in heaven," and attached to the word the notion of a supreme Divine Being. This word, with the spiritual idea corresponding to it, Moffat found to have vanished from the language of the present generation, although here and there he could meet with an old man, scarcely one or two in a thousand, who remembered in his youth to have heard speak of "Morimo:" and this word, once so deeply significant, only survived now in the spells and charms of the so-called rain-makers and sorcerers, who misused it to designate a fabulous ghost, of whom they told the absurdest and most contradictory things.

And as there is no such witness to the degradation of the savage as the brutal poverty of his language, so is there nothing that so effectually tends to keep him in the depths to which he has fallen. You can not impart to any man more than the words which he understands either now contain, or can be made intelligibly to him to contain. Language is as truly on one side the limit and restraint of thought, as on the other side that which feeds and unfolds it. Thus it is the ever-repeated complaint of the missionary that the very terms are wholly or nearly wholly wanting in the dialect of the savage whereby to impart to him heavenly truths, or indeed even the nobler emotions of the human heart. Dobrizhoffer, the Jesuit missionary, in his curious *History of the Abipones*, tells us that neither they nor the Guarinnies, two of the principal native tribes of Brazil, with whose languages he was intimately acquainted, possessed any word which in the least corresponded to our "thanks." But what wonder, if the feeling of gratitude was entirely absent from their hearts, that they should not have possessed the corresponding word in their vocabularies? Nay, how should they have had it there? And that this is the true explanation is plain from a fact which the same writer records, that although inveterate askers, they never showed the slightest sense of obligation or of gratitude, when they obtained what they sought; never saying more than, "This will be useful to me," or, "This is what I wanted."

Nor is it only in what they have forfeited and lost, but also in what they have retained or invented, that these languages proclaim their degradation and debasement, and how deeply they and those that speak them have fallen. Thus I have read of a tribe in New Holland, which has no word to signify God, but has a word to designate a process by which an unborn child is destroyed in the bosom of its mother. And I have been informed, on the authority of one excellently capable of knowing, an English scholar long resident in Van Diemen's Land, that in the native language of that island there are four words to express the taking of human life—one to express a father's killing of a son, another a son's killing of a father, with other varieties of murder; and that in no one of these lies the slightest moral reprobation, or sense of the deep-lying distinction between to kill and to murder; while at the same time, of that language so richly and so fearfully provided with expressions from this extremest utterance of hate, he also reports that any word for love is wanting in it altogether.

Yet with all this, ever and anon in the midst of this wreck and ruin there is that in the language of the savage, some subtle distinction, some curious allusion to a perished civilization, now utterly unintelligible to the speaker, or some other note, which proclaims his language to be the remains of a dissipated inheritance, the rags and remnants of a robe which was a royal one once. The fragments of a broken sceptre are in his hand, a sceptre wherewith once he held dominion (that is, in his progenitors) over large kingdoms of thought, which now have escaped wholly from his sway.

But while it is thus with him, while this is the downward course of all those that have chosen the downward path, while with every impoverishing and debasing of personal or national life there goes hand in hand a corresponding impoverishment and debasement of language, so on the contrary, where there is advance and progress, where a divine idea is in any measure realizing itself in a people, where they are learning more accurately to define and distinguish, more truly to know, where they are ruling, as men ought to rule, over nature, and making her to give up her secrets to them, where new thoughts are rising up over the horizon of a nation's mind, new feelings are stirring at a nation's heart, new facts coming within the sphere of its knowledge, there language is growing and advancing too. It can not lag behind; for man feels that nothing is properly his own, that he has not secured any new thought, or entered upon any new spiritual inheritance, till he has fixed it in language, till he can contemplate it, not as himself, but as his word; he is conscious that he must express truth, if he is to preserve it, and still more if he would propagate it among others. "Names," as it has been excellently said, "are impressions of sense, and as such take the strongest hold upon the mind, and of all other impressions can be most easily recalled and retained in view. They therefore serve to give a point of attachment to all the more volatile objects of thought and feeling. Impressions that when past might be dissipated for ever, are by their connection with language always within reach. Thoughts, of themselves, are perpetually slipping out of the field of immediate mental vision; but the name abides with us, and the utterance of it restores them in a moment." And on the necessity of names for the propagation of the truth it has been well observed: "Hardly any original thought on mental or social subjects ever make their way among mankind, or assume their proper importance in the minds even of their inventors, until aptly selected words or phrases have as it were nailed them down and held them fast."

Nor does what has here been said of the manner in which language enriches itself contradict a prior assertion that man starts with language as God's perfect gift, which he only impairs and forfeits by sloth and sin, according to the same law which holds good in respect of each other of the gifts of Heaven. For it was not meant, as indeed was then observed, that men would possess words to set forth feelings which were not yet stirring in them, combinations which they had not yet made, objects which they had not yet seen, relations of which they were not yet conscious; but that up to his needs (those needs including not merely his animal wants, but all his higher spiritual cravings), he would find utterance freely. The great logical, or grammatical framework of language (for grammar is the logic of speech, even as logic is the grammar of reason), he would possess, he knew not how; and certainly not as the final result of gradual acquisitions, but as that rather which alone had made those acquisitions possible; as that according to which he unconsciously worked, filling in this framework by degrees with these later acquisitions of thought, feeling, and experience, as one by one they arrayed themselves in the garment and vesture of words.

Here then is the explanation of the fact that language should be thus instructive for us, that it should yield us so much, when we come to analyze and probe it; and the more, the more deeply and accurately we do so. It is full of instruction, because it is the embodiment, the incarnation, if I may so speak, of the feelings and thoughts and experiences of a nation, yea, often of many nations, and of all which through centuries they have attained to and won. It stands like the pillars of Hercules, to mark how far the moral and intellectual conquests of mankind have advanced, only not like those pillars, fixed and immovable, but ever itself advancing with the progress of these; nay more—itself a great element of that advance; for "language is the armory of the human mind, and at once contains the trophies of its past and the weapons of its future conquests." The mighty moral instincts which have been working in the popular mind, have found therein their unconscious voice; and the single kinglier spirits that have looked deeper into the heart of things, have oftentimes gathered up all they have seen into some one word, which they have launched upon the world, and with which they have enriched it for ever—making in that new word a new region of thought to be henceforward in some sort the common heritage of all. Language is the amber in which a thousand precious and subtle thoughts have been safely embedded and preserved. It has arrested ten thousand lightning flashes of genius, which, unless thus fixed and arrested, might have been as bright, but would have also been as quickly passing and perishing, as the lightning. "Words convey the mental treasures of one period to the generations that follow; and laden with this, their precious freight, they sail safely across gulfs of time in which empires have suffered shipwreck, and the languages of common life have sunk into oblivion." And for all these reasons far more and mightier in every way is a language than any one of the works which may have been composed in it. For that work, great as it may be, is but the embodying of the mind of a single man, this of a nation. The *Iliad* is great, yet not so great in strength or power or beauty as the Greek language. *Paradise Lost* is a noble possession for a people to have inherited, but the English tongue is a nobler heritage yet.

Great then will be our gains, if, having these treasures of wisdom and knowledge lying round about us so far more precious than mines of California gold, we determine that we will make what portion of them we can our own, that we will ask the words we use to give an account of themselves, to say whence they are, and whither they tend. Then shall we often rub off the dust and rust from what seemed but a common token, which we had taken and given a thousand times, esteeming it no better, but which now we shall perceive to be a precious coin, bearing the "image and superscription" of the great king; then shall we often stand in surprise and in something of shame, while we behold the great spiritual realities which underlie our common speech, the marvellous truths which we have been witnessing *for* in our words, but, it may be, witnessing *against* in our lives. And as you will not find, for so I venture to promise, that this study of words will be a dull one when you undertake it yourselves, as little need you fear that it will prove dull and unattractive, when you seek to make your own gains herein the gains also of those who may be hereafter committed to your charge.

Only try your pupils, and mark the kindling of the eye, the lighting up of the countenance, the revival of the flagging attention, with which the humblest lecture upon words, and on the words especially which they are daily using, which are familiar to them in their play or at their church, will be welcomed by them. There is a sense of reality about children which makes them rejoice to discover that there is also a reality about words, that they are not merely arbitrary signs, but living powers; that, to reverse the words of one of England's "false prophets," they may be the fool's counters, but are the wise man's money; not like the sands of the sea, innumerable disconnected atoms, but growing out of roots, clustering in families, connecting and intertwining themselves with all that men have been doing and thinking and feeling from the beginning of the world till now.

And it is of course our English tongue, out of which mainly we should seek to draw some of the hid treasures which it contains, from which we should endeavor to remove the veil which custom and familiarity have thrown over it. We can not employ ourselves better. There is nothing that will more help to form an English heart in ourselves and in others than will this. We could scarcely have a single lesson on the growth of our English tongue, we could scarcely follow up one of its significant words, without having unawares a lesson in English history as well, without not merely falling on some curious fact illustrative of our national life, but learning also how the great heart which is beating at the centre of that life was gradually shaped and moulded. We should thus grow too in our feeling of connection with the past, of gratitude and reverence to it; we should estimate more truly, and therefore more highly, what it has done for us, all that it has bequeathed us, all that it has made ready to our hands. It was something for the children of Israel when they came into Canaan, to enter upon wells which they digged not, and vineyards which they had not planted, and houses which they had not built; but how much greater a boon, how much more glorious a prerogative, for any one generation to enter upon the inheritance of a language, which other generations by their truth and toil have made already a receptacle of choicest treasures, a storehouse of so much unconscious wisdom, a fit organ for expressing the subtlest distinctions, the tenderest sentiments, the largest thoughts, and the loftiest imaginations, which at any time the heart of men can conceive. And that those who have preceded us have gone far to accomplish this for us, I shall rejoice if I am able in any degree to make you feel in the lectures which will follow the present.

LECTURE II.

ON THE MORALITY IN WORDS.

Is man of a divine birth and stock? coming from God, and, when he fulfils the law and intention of his creation, returning to him again? We need no more than his language to prove it. So much is there in that which could never have existed on any other supposition. How else could all those words which testify of his relation to God, and of his consciousness of this relation, and which ground themselves thereon, have found their way into this, the veritable transcript of his innermost life, the genuine utterance of the faith and hope which is in him? On no other theory than this could we explain that great and preponderating weight thrown into the scale of goodness and truth, which, despite of all in the other scale, we must needs acknowledge in every language to be there. How else shall we account for that sympathy with the right, that testimony against the wrong, which, despite of all its aberrations and perversions, is yet its prevailing ground-tone?

But has man fallen, and deeply fallen, from the

heights of his original creation? We need no more than his language to prove it. Like everything else about him, it bears at once the stamp of his greatness and of his degradation, of his glory and of his shame. What dark and sombre threads he must have woven into the tissue of his life, before we could trace such dark ones running through the tissue of his language! What facts of wickedness and wo must have existed in the first, ere there could be such words to designate these as are found in the last. There have been always those who have sought to make light of the hurts which man has inflicted on himself, of the sickness with which he is sick; who would fain persuade themselves and others that moralists and divines, if they have not quite invented, have yet enormously exaggerated, these. But are these statements found only in scripture and in sermons? Are there not mournful corroborations of their truth imprinted deeply upon every region of man's natural and spiritual life, and on none more deeply than on his language? It needs no more than to open a dictionary, and to cast our eye thoughtfully down a few columns, and we shall find abundant confirmation of this sadder and sterner estimate of man's moral and spiritual condition. How else shall we explain this long catalogue of words, having all to do with sin, or with sorrow, or with both? How came they there? We may be quite sure that they were not invented without being needed, that they have each a correlative in the world of realities. I open the first letter of the alphabet; what means this "ah," this "alas," these deep and long-drawn sighs of humanity, which at once we encounter there? And then presently follow words such as these: "affliction," "agony," "anguish," "assassin," "atheist" "avarice," and twenty more—words, you will observe, for the most part not laid up in the recesses of the language, to be drawn forth and used at rare opportunities, but occupying many of them its foremost ranks. And indeed, as regards abundance, it is a melancholy thing to observe how much richer is every vocabulary in words that set forth sins, than in those that set forth graces. When St. Paul (Gal. v. 19–23) would put these against those, "the works of the flesh" against "the fruit of the Spirit," those are seventeen, these only nine; and where do we find in scripture such lists of graces, as we do at 2 Tim. iii. 2, Rom. i. 29–31, of their opposites?

Nor can I help taking note, in the oversight and muster from this point of view of the words which constitute a language, of the manner in which it has been put to all its resources that so it may express the infinite varieties, now of human suffering, now of human sin. Thus what a fearful thing is it that any language should have a word expressive of the pleasure which men feel at the calamities of others; for the existence of the word bears testimony to the existence of the thing. And yet in more than one such a word is found.* Nor are there wanting, I suppose, in any language, words which are the mournful record of the strange wickednesses which the genius of man, so fertile in evil has invented.

And our dictionaries, while they tell us much, yet will not tell us all. How shamefully rich is the language of the vulgar everywhere in words which are not allowed to find their way into books, yet which live as a sinful oral tradition on the lips of men, to set forth that which is unholy and impure. And of these words, as no less of those which have to do with the kindred sins of revelling and excess, how many set the evil forth with an evident sympathy and approbation, as taking part with the sin against Him who has forbidden it under pain of his extremest displeasure. How much wit, how much talent, yea, how much imagination must have stood in the service of sin, before it could have a nomenclature so rich, so varied, and often so Heaven-defying as it has.

How many words men have dragged downward with themselves, and made partakers more or less of their own fall. Having originally an honorable significance, they have yet, with the deterioration

* In the Greek, *ἐπιχαιρεκακία*, in the German, "Schadenfreude." Cicero so strongly feels that such a word is wanting, that he *gives* to "malevolentia" the same significance, "voluptas ex malo alterius," though it lies not of necessity in the word.

and degeneration of those that used them, deteriorated and degenerated too. What a multitude of words originally harmless, have assumed a harmful as their secondary meaning; how many worthy have acquired an unworthy. Thus "knave" meant once no more than lad (nor does it now in German mean more), "villain" than peasant; a "boor" was only a farmer, a "varlet" was but a serving-man, a "churl" but a strong fellow. "Time-server" was used two hundred years ago quite as often for one in an honorable as in a dishonorable sense "serving the time."* "Conceits" had once nothing conceited in them; "officious" had reference to offices of kindness and not of busy meddling; "moody" was that which pertained to a man's mood, without any gloom or sullenness implied. "Demure" (which is, "des mœurs," of good manners), conveyed no hint, as it does now, of an over-doing of the outward demonstrations of modesty. In "crafty" and "cunning" there was nothing of crooked wisdom implied, but only knowledge and skill; "craft," indeed, still retains very often its more honorable use, a man's "craft" being his skill, and then the trade in which he is well skilled. And think you that the Magdalen could have ever given us "maudlin" in its present contemptuous application, if the tears of penitential weeping had been held in due honor in the world? "Tinsel," from the French "étincelle,"

* See in proof Fuller's *Holy State*, b. iii. c. 19.

meant once anything that sparkles or glistens; thus "cloth of tinsel" would be cloth inwrought with silver and gold; but the sad experience that "all is not gold that glitters," that much which shows fair and specious to the eye is yet worthless in reality, has caused the word imperceptibly to assume the meaning which it now has, and when we speak of "tinsel," either literally or figuratively, we always mean now that which has no reality of sterling worth underlying the glittering and specious shows which it makes. "Tawdry," which is a word of curious derivation, though I will not pause to go into it, has undergone exactly the same process; it once conveyed no intimation of *mean* finery, or *shabby* splendor, as now it does.

A like deterioration through use may be traced in the word "to resent." It was not very long ago that Barrow could speak of the good man as a faithful "resenter" and requiter of benefits, of the duty of testifying an affectionate "resentment" of our obligations to God. But, alas! the memory of benefits fades and fails from us so much more quickly than that of injuries; that which we afterward remember and revolve in our minds is so much more predominantly the wrongs real or imaginary which men have done us, than the favors they have bestowed on us, that "to resent" in our modern English has come to be confined entirely to that deep reflective displeasure which men entertain against those that have done, or whom they believe to have done, them a wrong. And this leads us to inquire how it comes to pass that we do not speak of the "retaliation" of benefits, as often as the "retaliation" of injuries? The word does but signify the again rendering as much as we have received; but this is so much seldomer thought of in regard of benefits than of wrongs, that the word, though not altogether unused in this its worthier sense, has yet a strange and somewhat unusual sound in our ears when so employed. Were we to speak of a man "retaliating" kindnesses, I am not sure that every one would understand us.

Neither is it altogether satisfactory to take note that "animosity," according to its derivation, means no more than "spiritedness;" that in the first use of the word in the later Latin to which it belongs, it was employed in this sense; was applied, for instance, to the spirit and fiery courage of the horse; but that now it is applied to only one kind of vigor and activity, that namely which is displayed in enmity and hate, and expresses a spiritedness in these. Does not this look too much as if these oftenest stirred men to a lively and vigorous activity?

And then what a mournful witness for the hard and unrighteous judgments we habitually form of one another lies in the word "prejudice." The word of itself means plainly no more than "a judgment formed beforehand," without affirming anything as to whether that judgment be favorable or unfavorable to the person about whom it is formed. Yet so predominantly do we form harsh, unfavorable judgments of others before knowledge and experience, that a "prejudice," or judgment before knowledge and not grounded on evidence, is almost always taken to signify an unfavorable anticipation about one; and "prejudicial" has actually acquired a secondary meaning of anything which is mischievous or injurious.

As these words are a testimony to the *sin* of man, so there is a signal testimony to his *infirmity*, to the limitation of human faculties and human knowledge, in the word "to retract." To retract means properly, as its derivation declares, no more than to handle over again, to reconsider. And yet, so certain are we to find in a subject which we reconsider or handle a second time, that which was at the first rashly, inaccurately stated, that which needs therefore to be amended, modified, withdrawn; that "to retract" could not tarry long with its primary meaning of reconsidering; and has come to signify, as we commonly use it, "to withdraw." Thus a great writer of the Latin church, at the close of his life wishing to amend whatever he might now perceive in his various published works to have been incautiously or incorrectly stated, gave to the book in which he carried out this intention (for they had then no such opportunities as second and third editions afford now) this very name of "Retractations," being strictly "Rehandlings," but in fact, as any one turning to the work will at once perceive, withdrawings of various statements, which he now considered to need thus to be withdrawn. What a seal does this word's acquisition of such a secondary use as this set to the proverb, *humanum est errare.*

At the same time urging, as I have thus done, this degeneration of words, I should greatly err, if I failed to bring before you the fact that a parallel process of purifying and ennobling has also been going forward, especially, through the influences of Divine faith working in the world; which, as it has turned *men* from evil to good, or lifted them from a lower earthly goodness to a higher heavenly, so has it in like manner elevated, purified, and ennobled a multitude of the words which they employ, until these which once expressed only an earthly good, express now a heavenly. The gospel of Christ, as it is the redemption of man, so is it in a multitude of instances the redemption of his word, freeing it from the bondage of corruption, that it should no longer be subject to vanity, nor stand any more in the service of sin or of the world, but in the service of God and of his truth. In the Greek language there is a word for "humility;" but this humility meant for the Greek —that is, with very rarest exceptions—meanness of spirit. He who brought in the Christian grace of humility did in so doing rescue also the word which expressed it for nobler uses, and to a far higher dignity than hitherto it had attained. There were "angels" before heaven had been opened, but these only earthly messengers; "martyrs" also, or witnesses, but these not unto blood, nor yet for God's highest truth; "apostles," but sent of men; "evangels," but not of the kingdom of heaven; "advocates," but not "with the Father." "Paradise" was a word common in slightly different forms to almost all the nations of the East; but they meant by it only some royal park or garden of delights; till for the Jew it was exalted to signify the wondrous abode of our first parents; and higher honors awaited it still, when, on the lips of the Lord, it signified the blissful waiting-place of faithful departed souls (Luke xxiii. 43); yea, the heavenly blessedness itself (Rev. ii. 7). Nor was the word "regeneration" unknown to the Greeks: they could speak of the earth's regeneration in the spring-time, of memory as the regeneration of knowledge; the Jewish historian could describe the return of his countrymen from the Babylonian captivity, and their re-establishment under Cyrus in their own land, as the regeneration of the Jewish state; but still the word, on the lips of either Jew or Greek, was very far removed from that honor reserved for it in the Christian dispensation —namely, that it should be the bearer of one of the chiefest and most blessed mysteries of the faith. And many other words in like manner there are "fetched from the very dregs of paganism,"* as one has said, which words the Holy Spirit has not refused to employ for the setting forth of the great truths of our redemption. Reversing in this the impious deed of Belshazzar, who profaned the sacred vessels of God's house to sinful and idolatrous uses (Dan. v. 2), that blessed Spirit has often consecrated the very idol vessels of Babylon to the service of the sanctuary.

Let us now proceed to contemplate some of the attestations for God's truth, and then some of the playings into the hands of the devil's falsehood, which may be found to lurk in words. And first, the witnesses to God's truth, the falling in of our words with his unchangeable word: for these, as the true uses of the word, while the other are only its abuses, have a prior claim to be considered. Some modern false prophets, who would gladly explain away all the phenomena of the world around us, as declare man to be a sinful being and enduring the consequences of sin, tell us that pain is only a subordinate kind of pleasure, or at worst that it is a sort of needful hedge and guardian of pleasure. But there is deeper feeling in the universal heart of man, bearing witness to something very different from this shallow explanation of the existence of pain in the present econo-

* Sanderson, Sermons, 1671, v. 2, p. 124. He instances the Latin "sacrament," the Greek "mystery."

my of the world—namely, that it is the correlative of sin, that it is *punishment;* and to this the word "pain," which there can be no reasonable doubt is derived from "pœna," bears continual witness. Pain *is* punishment; so does the word itself, no less than the conscience of every one that is suffering it, declare. Just so, again, there are those who will not hear of great pestilences being God's scourges of men's sins; who fain would find out natural causes for them, and account for them by the help of these. I remember it was thus with too many during both our fearful visitations from the cholera. They may do so, or imagine that they do so; yet every time they use the word "plague," they implicitly own the fact which they are endeavoring to deny; for "plague" means properly and according to its derivation, "blow," or "stroke;" and was a title given to these terrible diseases, because the great universal conscience of men, which is never at fault, believed and confessed that these were "strokes" or "blows" inflicted by God on a guilty and rebellious world. With reference to such words so used we may truly say: *Vox populi, vox Dei,* The voice of the people is the voice of God—a proverb which shallowly interpreted may be made to contain a most mischievous falsehood; but interpreted in the sense wherein no doubt it was spoken, holds a deepest truth. We must only remember that this "people" is not the populace either in high place or in low;

and that this "voice of the people" is not any momentary outcry, but the consenting testimony of the good and wise, of those neither brutalized by ignorance, nor corrupted by a false cultivation, in all places and in all times.

Every one who admits the truth which lies in this saying must, I think, acknowledge it as a remarkable fact, that men should have agreed to apply the word "miser," or miserable, to the man eminently addicted to the vice of covetousness, to him who loves his money with his whole heart and soul. Here, too, the moral instinct lying deep in all hearts has borne testimony to the tormenting nature of this vice, to the gnawing cares with which even here it punishes him that entertains it, to the enmity which there is between it and all joy; and the man who enslaves himself to his money is proclaimed in our very language to be a "miser," or a miserable man.*

How deep an insight into the failings of the human heart lies at the root of many words; and if only we would attend to them, what valuable warnings many contain against subtle temptations and sins! Thus, all of us have probably, more or less, felt the temptation of seeking to please others by an unmanly assenting to their view of some matter, even when our own independent convictions would lead us to a different.

* We here in fact say in a word what the Roman moralist, when he wrote, "Nulla avaritia sine pœnâ est, *quamvis satis sit ipsa pœnarum*," took a sentence to say.

The existence of such a temptation, and the fact that too many yield to it, are both declared in a Latin word for a flatterer — "assentator" — that is, "an assenter;" one who has not courage to say No, when a Yes is expected from him: and quite independently of the Latin, the German language, in its contemptuous and precisely equivalent use of "Jaherr," or "a yea Lord," warns us in like manner against all such unmanly compliances. I may observe by the way that we also once possessed the word "assentation" in the sense of unworthy, flattering lip-assent; the last example of it which Richardson gives is from Bishop Hall: "It is a fearful presage of ruin when the prophets conspire in *assentation*." The word is quite worthy to be revived. Again, how good it is to have that spirit of depreciation of others, that willingness to find spots and stains in the characters of the greatest and the best, that so they may not oppress and rebuke us with a goodness and greatness so far surpassing ours — to have this tendency met and checked by a word at once so expressive, and one which we should so little like to take home to ourselves, as the French "dénigreur." This word also is now I believe out of use; which is a pity, while yet the thing is everywhere so frequent. Full too of instruction and warning is our present employment of the word "libertine." It signified, according to its earliest use in French and in English, a speculative free-thinker in matters of religion, and in the theory of morals, or, it might be, of government. But as by a sure process free-*thinking* does and will end in free-*acting*, as he who has cast off the one yoke, will cast off the other, so a "libertine" came in two or three generations to signify a profligate, especially in relation to women, a licentious and debauched person.

There is much, too, that we may learn from looking a little closely at the word "passion." We sometimes think of the "passionate" man as a man of strong will, and of real though ungoverned energy. But this word declares to us most plainly the contrary; for it, as a very solemn use of it declares, means properly "suffering;" and a passionate man is not a man doing something, but one suffering something to be done on him. When, then, a man or child is "in a passion," this is no coming out in him of a strong will, of a real energy, but rather the proof that for the time at least he has no will, no energy; he is suffering, not doing — suffering his anger, or what other evil temper it may be, to lord over him without control. Let no one then think of passion as a sign of strength. As reasonably might one assume that it was a proof of a man being a strong man that he was often well beaten. Such a fact would be evidence that a strong man was putting forth his strength on him, but of anything rather than that he himself was strong. The same sense of passion and feebleness going together, of the first being born of the second, lies, as I may remark by the way, in the two-fold use of the Latin word, *impotens* —which, meaning first weak, means then violent; and then often weak and violent together.

In our use of the word "talents," as when we say, "a man of talents" (not of "talent," for that, as we shall see presently, is nonsense), there is a clear recognition of the responsibilities which go along with the possession of intellectual gifts and endowments, whatsoever they may be. We draw, beyond a doubt, the word from the parable in scripture in which various talents, more and fewer, are committed to the several servants by their lord, that they may trade with them in his absence, and give account of their employment at his return. Men may choose to forget the ends for which their talents were given them; they may turn them to selfish ends; they may glorify themselves in them, instead of glorifying the Giver; they may practically deny that they were given at all; yet in this word, till they can rid their vocabulary of it, abides a continual memento that they were so given, or rather lent, and that each man shall have to render an account of their use.

Let us a little consider the word "kind." We speak of a "kind" person, and we speak of man-"kind," and perhaps, if we think about the matter at all, we seem to ourselves to be using quite different words, or the same word in senses quite unconnected, and having no bond between them. But they are connected, and that most closely; a "kind" person is a "kinned" person, one of kin; one who acknowledges and acts upon his kinship with other men, confesses that he owes to them, as of one blood with himself, the debt of love. And so man*kind* is man *kinned*.* In the word is contained a declaration of the relationship which exists between all the members of the human family; and seeing that this relationship in a race now scattered so widely and divided so far asunder can only be through a common head, we do in fact every time that we use the word "mankind," declare our faith in the one common descent of the whole race of man. And beautiful before, how much more beautiful now do the words "kind" and "kindness" appear, when we perceive the root out of which they grow; that they are the acknowledgment in deeds of love of our kinship with our brethren; and how profitable to keep in mind that a lively recognition of the bonds of blood, whether of those closer ones which unite us to that whom by best right we term our family, or those wider ones which knit us to the whole human family, that this is the true source out of which all genuine love and affection must spring; for so much is affirmed in our daily, hourly use of the word.

And other words there are, having reference to the family and the relations of family life, which are

* Thus it is not a mere play upon words, but something much deeper, which Shakspere puts into Hamlet's mouth; when speaking of his father's brother who had married his mother, he characterizes him as "A little more than *kin* and less than *kind*."

not less full of teaching, which each may serve to remind of some duty. For example, "husband" is properly "house-band," the *band* and *bond* of the house, who shall bind and hold it together. Thus, Old Tusser in his *Points of Husbandry*:—

> "The name of the *husband* what is it to say?
> Of wife and of *house*hold the *band* and the stay:"

so that the very name may put him in mind of his authority, and of that which he ought to be to all the members of the house. And the name "wife" has its lessons too, although not so deep a one as the equivalent word in some other tongues. It belongs to the same family of words as "weave," "woof," "web," and the German, "weben." It is a title given to her who is engaged at the web and woof, these having been the most ordinary branches of female industry, of wifely employment, when the language was forming. So that in the word itself is wrapped up a hint of earnest in-door stay-at-home occupations, as being the fittest for her who bears this name.

But it was observed just now that there are also words which bear the slime on them of the serpent's trail; and the uses of words, which imply moral perversity—I say not upon their parts who now employ them in the senses which they have acquired, but on theirs from whom little by little they received their deflection, and were warped from their original rectitude. Thus for instance is it with the word "prude," signifying as now it does a woman with an over-scrupulous affectation of a modesty which she does not really feel, and betraying the absence of the reality by this over-preciseness and niceness about the shadow. This use of the word must needs have been the result of a great corruption of manners in them among whom it grew up. Goodness must have gone strangely out of fashion, before things could have come to this. For "prude," which is a French word, means virtuous or prudent; "prud'homme" being a man of courage and probity. But where morals are greatly and almost universally relaxed, virtue is often treated as hypocrisy; and thus, in a dissolute age, and one disbelieving the existence of any inward purity, the word "prude" came to designate one who affected a virtue, even as none were esteemed to do anything more; and in this use of it, which, having once acquired, it continues to retain, abides an evidence of the corrupt world's dislike to and disbelief in the realities of goodness, its willingness to treat them as mere hypocrisies and shows.

Again, why should the word "simple" be used slightingly, and "simpleton" more slightingly still? According to its derivation the "simple," is one "without fold," sine plicâ; just what we may imagine Nathanael to have been, and what our Lord attributed as the highest honor to him, the "Israelite without guile;" and indeed, what higher honor could there be than to have nothing double about us, to be without duplicities or folds? Even the world, that despises "simplicity," does not profess to approve of "duplicity," or double-foldedness. But inasmuch as we feel that in a world like ours such a man will make himself a prey, is likely to prove no match for the fraud and falsehood which he will everywhere encounter, and as there is that in most men which, if they were obliged to choose between deceiving and being deceived, would make them choose the former, it has come to pass that "simple," which in a world of righteousness would be a word of highest honor, implies here in this world of ours, something of scorn for the person to whom it is applied. And must it not be confessed to be a striking fact that exactly in the same way a person of deficient intellect is called an "innocent," *in nocens*, one that does not hurt? so that this word assumes that the first and chief use men make of their intellectual powers will be to do hurt, that where they are wise, it will be to do evil. What a witness does human language bear here against human sin!

Nor are these isolated examples of the contemptuous application of words expressive of goodness. They meet us on every side. Thus "silly," written "seely" in our earlier English, is beyond a doubt the German "selig," which means "blessed." We see the word in its transition state in our early poets, with whom "silly" is so often an affectionate epithet, applied to sheep as expressive of their harmlessness and innocency. With a still slighter departure from its original meaning, an early English poet applies the word to the Lord of Glory himself, while yet an infant of days, styling him "this harmless *silly* babe." But here the same process went forward as with the words "simple" and "innocent." And the same moral phenomenon repeats itself continually. For example: at the first promulgation of the Christian faith, and while yet the name of its Divine Founder was somewhat new and strange to the ears of the heathen, they were wont, some perhaps out of ignorance, but more of intention, slightly to mispronounce this name, as though it had not been "Christus," but "Chrestus," that word signifying in Greek "benevolent," or "benign." That they who did it of intention meant no honor hereby to the Lord of Life, but the contrary, is certain; and indeed the word, like the "silly," "innocent," "simple," of which we have already spoken, had already contracted a slight tinge of contempt, or else there would have been no inducement to fasten it on the Savior. What a strange shifting of the moral sense there must have been, before it could have done so before men could have found in a name implying benignity and goodness a nickname of scorn. The French have their "bonhommie" with the same undertone of contempt, the Greeks also a well-known word. It is to the honor of the Latin, and is very characteristic of the best side of Roman life, that "simplex" and "simplicitas" never acquired this abusive signification.

Again, we all know how prone men are to ascribe to chance or fortune those good gifts and blessings which indeed come directly from God—to build altars to fortune rather than to Him who is the author of every good thing. And this faith of theirs, that their blessings, even their highest, come to them by a blind chance, they have incorporated in a word; for "happy" and "happiness" are of course connected with and derived from "hap," which is chance. But how unworthy is this word to express any true felicity, of which the very essence is that it excludes hap or chance, that the world neither gave it nor can take it away. It is indeed *more* objectionable than "lucky" and "fortunate," objectionable as also are these, inasmuch as by the "happy" man we mean much more than by the "fortunate." Very nobly has a great English poet protested against the misuse of the latter word, when of one who had lost indeed everything beside, but, as he esteemed, had kept the truth, he exclaims:—

> "Call not the royal Swede *unfortunate*,
> Who never did to *fortune* bend the knee."

But another way in which the immorality of words mainly displays itself, one, too, in which perhaps they work their greatest mischief, is that of giving honorable names to dishonorable things, making sin plausible by dressing it out sometimes even in the very colors of goodness, or if not so, yet in such as go far to conceal its own native deformity. "The tongue," as St. James has declared, "is a *world* of iniquity" (iii. 6); or as some interpreters affirm the words ought rather to be translated, and they would be then still more to our purpose, "*the ornament* of iniquity," that which sets it out in fair and attractive colors: and those who understand the original will at once perceive that such a meaning may possibly lie in the words. On the whole I do not believe that these expositors are right, yet certainly the connection of the Greek word for "tongue" with our "gloze," "glossy," with the German "gleissen," to smoothe over or polish, with an obsolete Greek word as well, also signifying "to polish," is not accidental, but real, and may well suggest some searching thoughts, as to the uses whereunto we turn this "*best*," but, as it may therefore prove also, this *worst* "member that we have."

How much wholesomer on all accounts is it that there should be an ugly word for an ugly thing, one involving moral condemnation and disgust, even at the expense of a little coarseness, rather than one which plays fast and loose with the eternal principles of morality, which makes sin plausible, and shifts the divinely-reared landmarks of right and wrong, thus bringing the user under the wo of them "that call evil good, and good evil, that put darkness for light, and light for darkness, that put sweet for bitter, and bitter for sweet" (Isa. v. 20) — a text on which South has written four of his greatest sermons, with reference to this very matter, and bearing this striking title, *On the fatal imposture and force of words.* How awful, yea, how fearful, is this force and imposture of theirs, leading men captive at will. There is an atmosphere about them which they are evermore diffusing, an atmosphere of life or death, which we insensibly inhale at each moral breath we draw.* "The winds of the soul," as one called them of old, they fill its sails, and are continually impelling it upon its course, heavenward or to hell. How immense is the difference as to the light in which we shall learn to regard a sin, according as we have been wont to designate and to hear it designated by a word which brings out its loathsomeness and deformity;—or by one which conceals these; as when in Italy, during the period that poisoning was rifest, nobody was said to be poisoned; it was only that the death of some was "assisted" (aiutata); or again, by one which seeks to turn the edge of the Divine threatenings against it by a jest; as when in France a subtle poison, by which impatient heirs delivered themselves from

* Bacon's words have been often quoted, but they will bear being quoted once more: "Credunt enim homines rationem suam verbis imperare. Sed fit etiam ut verba vim suam super intellectum retorqueant et reflectant."

those who stood between them and the inheritance which they coveted, was called "poudre de succession;" or, worse than all, which shall throw a flimsy vail of sentiment over it. As an example of the last, what a source of mischief in all our country parishes is the one practice of calling a child born out of wedlock, a "love-child" instead of a bastard. It would be hard to estimate how much it has lowered the tone and standard of morality among us; or for how many young women it may have helped to make the downward way more sloping still. How vigorously ought we to oppose ourselves to all such immoralities of language; which opposition will yet never be easy or pleasant; for many that will endure to commit a sin, will resent having that sin called by its right name.*

Coarse as, according to our present usages of lan-

* On the general subject of the reaction of a people's language on that people's moral life, I will adduce some words of Milton, who, as he did so much to enlarge, to enrich, to purify our mother tongue, so also in the Latin which he wielded so well, has thus declared his mind: "Neque enim qui sermo, purusne an corruptus, quæve loquendi proprietas quotidiana populo sit, parvi interesse arbitrandum est, quæ res Athenis non semel saluti fuit; immo vero, quod Platonis sententia est, immutato vestiendi more habituque graves in Republicâ motus mutationesque portendi, equidem potius collabente in vitium atque errorem loquendi usu occasum ejus urbis remque humilem et obscuram subsequi crediderim: verba enim partim inscita et putida, partim mendosa et perperam prolata, quid si ignavos et oscitantes et ad servile quidvis jam olim paratos incolarum animos haud levi indicio declarant? Contra nullum unquam audivimus imperium, nullam civitatem non mediocriter saltem floruisse, quamdiu linguæ sua gratia, suusque cultus constitit." Compare an interesting epistle (the 114th) of Seneca.

guage, may be esteemed the word by which our plain-speaking Anglo-Saxon fathers were wont to designate the unhappy women who make a trade of selling their bodies to the lusts of men, yet is there a profound moral sense in that word, bringing prominently out, as it does, the true vileness of their occupation, who for *hire* are content to profane and lay waste the deepest sanctities of their life. Consider the truth which is witnessed for here, as compared with the falsehood of many other titles by which they have been known—names which may themselves be called "whited sepulchres," so fair are they without, yet hiding so much foul within; as for instance, that in the French language which ascribes *joy* to a life which more surely than any other dries up all the sources of gladness in the heart, brings anguish, astonishment, blackest melancholy, on all who have addicted themselves to it. In the same way how much more moral words are the English "sharper," and "blackleg," than the French "chevalier d'industrie:" and the same holds good of the English equivalent, coarse as it is, for the Latin "conciliatrix." In this last word we have a notable example of the putting of bitter for sweet, and darkness for light, of the attempt to present a disgraceful occupation on an amiable, almost a sentimental side, rather than in its own true deformity and ugliness.*

* So conscious have men been of this tendency of theirs to throw the mantle of an honorable word over a dishonorable thing, or *vice*

If I wanted any further proof of this which I have been urging, namely, the moral atmosphere which words diffuse, I would ask you to observe how the first thing which men will do, when engaged in controversy with others, be it in the conflict of the tongue or the pen, or of weapons sharper yet, if sharper there be, will be to assume some honorable name to themselves, which, if possible, begs the whole matter in dispute, and at the same time to affix on their adversaries a name which shall place them in an invidious, or a ridiculous, or a contemptible, or an odious light. There is a deep instinct in men, deeper perhaps than they give any account of to themselves, which tells them how far this will go; that multitudes, utterly unable to weigh the arguments of the case, will yet be receptive of the influences which these words continually, though almost imperceptibly, diffuse. By arguments they might hope to gain over the reason of a few, but by these they enlist what at first are so much more effectual,

versâ, of the temptation to degrade an honorable thing, when they do not love it, by a dishonorable appellation, that the Greek language has a word significative of this very attempt, and its great moral teachers frequently occupy themselves in detecting this most frequent, yet perhaps practically most mischievous, among all the impostures of words — *ὑποκορίζεσθαι*, itself a word with an interesting history. And when Thucydides (iii. 82) would paint the fearful moral deterioration of Greece in the progress of its great Civil War, he adduces this alteration of the received value of words, this fitting of false names to everything — names of honor to the base, and of baseness to the honorable — as one of its most striking signs, even as it again set forward the evil, of which it had been first the result the passions and prejudices of many, on their side. Thus when at the beginning of our Civil Wars the parliamentary party styled themselves "The Godly," and the royalists "The Malignants," it is very certain that wherever they could procure entrance for these words, the question upon whose side the right lay was already decided. I do not adduce this instance as at all implying that the royalists did not make exactly the same employment of question-begging words, and of words steeped quite as deeply in the passion which animated them, but only as a sufficient illustration of my meaning.

Seeing, then, that language contains so faithful a record of the good and of the evil which in time past have been working in the minds and hearts of men, we should not err if we regard it as a moral barometer, which indicates and permanently marks the rise or fall of a nation's life. To study a people's language will be to study *them*, and to study them at best advantage, where they present themselves to us under fewest disguises, most nearly as they are. Too many have had a hand in it, and in causing it to arrive at its present shape, it is too entirely the collective work of the whole nation, the result of the united contributions of all, it obeys too immutable laws, to allow any successful tampering with it, any making of it to witness other than the actual facts of the case.

The frivolity of an age or nation, its mockery of

itself, its inability to comprehend the true dignity and meaning of life, the feebleness of its moral indignation, all this will find an utterance in the use of solemn and earnest words in senses comparatively trivial or even ridiculous, in the squandering of such as ought to have been reserved for the highest mysteries of the spiritual life on slight and secular objects, in the employment almost in jest and play of words implying the deepest moral guilt—as for instance the French 'perfide;' while, on the contrary, the high sentiment, the scorn of everything mean or base of another people or time, will as certainly in one way or another stamp themselves on the words which they employ; and thus, too, with whatever good or evil they may own.

Often a people's use of some single word will afford us a deeper insight into their real condition, their habits of thought and feeling, than whole volumes written expressly with the intention of imparting this insight. Thus our word "idiot" is abundantly characteristic, not indeed of English, but of Greek life, from which we have derived it and our use of it. The ἰδιώτης or "idiot" was in its earliest usage the private man, as contradistinguished from him who was clothed with some office and had a share in the management of public affairs. In this its primary use it is occasionally employed in English; as in Jeremy Taylor, who says, "Humility is a duty in great ones as well as in idiots." It came then to signify a rude, ignorant, unskilled, intellectually-unexercised person, a boor; this derivation or secondary sense bearing witness, as has been most truly said, to "the Greek notion of the indispensableness of public life, even to the right development of the intellect,"* a feeling which was entirely inwoven in the Greek habit of thought, lying at the foundation of all schemes of mental culture. Nor is it easy to see how it could have uttered itself with greater clearness than it does in this secondary use of the word "idiot." Our tertiary, according to which the "idiot" is one deficient in intellect, and not merely one with its powers unexercised, is but this secondary pushed a little further. Again, the innermost distinction between the Greek mind and the Hebrew reveal themselves in the several salutations of each, the "rejoice" of the first, the "peace" of the second. The clear, cheerful, world-enjoying temper of the Greek embodies itself in the first; he could desire nothing better or higher for himself, and thus could not wish it for his friend, than to have joy in his life. But the Hebrew had a deeper longing within him, and one which finds utterance in his "peace." It is not hard to perceive why this people should have been chosen as the first bearers of that truth which indeed enables truly to *rejoice*, but only through first bringing *peace;* nor why from them the word of life should first go forth. It

* Archdeacon Hare's *Mission of the Comforter*, p. 552.

may be urged, indeed, that these were only forms, and so in great part they may have at length become; as in our "good-by" or "adieu" we can hardly be said now to commit our friend to the Divine protection; yet still they were not such at the first, nor would they have held their ground, if ever they had become such altogether.

So, too, the modifications of meaning which a word has undergone, as it had been transplanted from one soil to another, the way in which one nation receiving a word from another, has yet brought into it some new force which was foreign to it in the tongue whence it was borrowed, has deepened, or extenuated, or otherwise altered its meaning—all this may prove profoundly instructive, and may reveal to us, as perhaps nothing else would, the most fundamental diversities existing between them. Observe, for instance, how different is the word "self-sufficient" as used by us, and by the heathen nations of antiquity. The Greek work exactly corresponding to it is a word of honor, and applied to men in their praise. And indeed it was the glory of the heathen philosophy to teach a man to find his resources in his own bosom, to be thus sufficient for himself; and seeing that a true centre without him and above him, a centre in God, had not been revealed to him, it was no shame for him to seek it there; better this, such as it was, than no centre at all. But the gospel has taught us another lesson, to find our sufficiency in God: and thus "self-sufficient," which with the Greek was a word in honorable use, is not so with us. Self-sufficiency is not a quality which any man desires now to be attributed to him. We have a feeling about the word, which causes it to carry its own condemnation with it; and its different uses, for honor once, for reproach now, do in fact ground themselves on the central differences of heathenism and Christianity.

Once more, we might safely conclude that a nation would not be likely tamely to submit to tyranny and wrong, which had made "quarrel" out of "querela." The Latin word means properly "complaint," and we have in "querulous" this its proper meaning coming distinctly out. Not so however in "quarrel;" for Englishmen, having been wont not merely to complain, but to set vigorously about righting and redressing themselves, their griefs being also grievances, out of this word, which might have given them only "querulous" and "querulousness," they have gotten "quarrel" as well.

On the other hand we can not wonder that Italy should fill our Great Exhibition with beautiful specimens of her skill in the arts, with statues and sculptures of rare loveliness, but should only rivet her chains the more closely by the weak and ineffectual efforts which she makes to break them, when she can degrade the word "virtuoso," or "the virtuous," to signify one accomplished in painting, music, and sculpture, such things as are the ornamental fringe of a nation's life, but can never be made, without loss of all manliness of character, its main texture and woof—not to say that excellence in these fine arts has been in too many cases divorced from all true virtue and worth. And what shall we say concerning the uses to which she turns her "bravo"? The opposite exaggeration of the ancient dwellers in Italy, who often made "virtus" to signify warlike courage alone, as if for them all virtues were included in this one, was at all events more tolerable than this; for there is a sense in which a man's "valor" is his value. How little, again, the modern Italians live in the spirit of their ancient worthies, or reverence the greatest among them, we may argue from the fact that they have been content to take the name of one among their noblest, and degrade it so far that every glib and loquacious hireling who shows strangers about their picture galleries, palaces, and ruins, is termed by them a "Cicerone," or a Cicero! So too the French use of the word "honnêteté," as external civility, marks a tendency to accept the shows and pleasant courtesies of social life in the room of deeper moral qualities.

How much too may be learned by noting the words which nations have been obliged to borrow from other nations, as not having them of home-growth — this, in general, if not in every case, testifying that the thing itself was not native, was only an exotic, transplanted, like the word which indicated it, from a foreign soil. Thus it is singularly characteristic of the social and political life of England, as distinguished from that of the other European nations, that to it alone the word "clubs" belongs; that the French and German languages have been alike unable to grow a word of their own as its equivalent, and have both been obliged to borrow this from us. And no wonder; for these voluntary associations of men for the furthering of such social or political ends as are near to the hearts of the associates could have only had their rise under such favorable circumstances as ours. In no country where there was not extreme personal freedom could they have sprung up; and as little in any where men did not know how to use this freedom with moderation and self-restraint, could they long have been endured. It was comparatively easy to adopt the word; but the ill success of the "club" itself everywhere save here where it is native, has shown that it was not so easy to transplant the thing. While we have lent this and other words, mostly political, to the French and to the German, it would not be less instructive, were this a suitable opportunity, to trace our corresponding obligations to them.

But it is time to bring this lecture to an end. These illustrations, to which it would not be hard to add many more, are amply enough to justify what

I have asserted of the existence of a moral element in words; they are enough to make us feel about them, that they do not hold themselves neutral in the great conflict between good and evil, light and darkness, which is dividing the world; that they are not contented to be the passive vehicles, now of the truth, and now of falsehood. We see on the contrary that they continually take their side, are some of them children of light, others children of this world, or even of darkness; they beat with the pulses of our life; they stir with our passions; they receive from us the impressions of our good and of our evil, which again they are active further to propagate among us. Must we not own, then, that there is a wondrous and mysterious world, of which we may hitherto have taken too little account, around us and about us? and may there not be a deeper meaning than hitherto we have attached to it, lying in that solemn declaration, "By thy words thou shalt be justified, and by thy words thou shalt be condemned"?

LECTURE III.

THE HISTORY IN WORDS.

It might at first sight appear as if language, apart that is from literature and books, and where these did not exist, was the frailest, the most untrustworthy, of all the vehicles of knowledge, and that most likely to betray its charge: yet is it in fact the great, oftentimes the only, connecting link between the present and the remotest past, an ark riding above waterfloods that have swept away every other landmark and memorial of ages and generations. Far beyond all written records in a language, the language itself stretches back and offers itself for our investigation — "the pedigree of nations," as Johnson calls it — itself a far more ancient monument and document than any writing which it contains. These records, moreover, may have been falsified by carelessness, by vanity, by fraud, by a multitude of causes; but *it* is never false, never deceives us, if we know how to question it aright.

And this questioning of it will often lead to conclusions of extreme importance. Thus there have been those who have denied on one ground or another the accuracy of the Scripture statement that the whole earth was peopled from a single pair; who have sought to prove that there must have been many beginnings, many centres. In answer to these, the *physical* unity of the race of mankind has been triumphantly shown by Dr. Prichard and others; but all recent investigations plainly announce that a yet stronger evidence, and a moral argument more convincing still, for the unity of mankind will be found in the proofs which are daily accumulating of the tendency of all languages, however widely they may differ now, to refer themselves to a common stock and single fountain-head. Of course we need not these proofs, who believe the fact, because it is written; yet can we only rejoice at each new homage which Science pays to revealed Truth, being sure that at the last she will stand in her service altogether.

Such investigations as these, however, lie plainly out of your sphere. Not so, however, those humbler, yet not less interesting inquiries, which by the aid of any tolerable dictionary you may carry on into the past history of your own land, as born witness to by the present language of its people, on which language the marks and vestiges of great revolutions are visibly and profoundly impressed, never again to be obliterated from it. You know how the geologist is able from the different strata and deposites, primary, secondary, or tertiary, succeeding one another, which he meets, to conclude the successive physical changes through which a region has passed; is in a condition to preside at those changes, to measure the forces which were at work to produce them, and almost to indicate their date. Now with such a composite language as the English before us, we may carry on moral and historical researches precisely analogous to his. Here too are strata and deposites, not of gravel and chalk, sandstone and limestone, but of Celtic, Latin, Saxon, Danish, Norman, and then again Latin and French words, with slighter intrusions from other sources: and any one with skill to analyze the language might re-create for himself the history of the people speaking that language, might come to appreciate the divers elements out of which that people was composed, in what proportion these were mingled, and in what succession they followed one upon the other.

Take for example the relation in which the Saxon and Norman occupants of this land stood to one another. I doubt not that an account of this, in the main as accurate as it would be certainly instructive, might be drawn from an intelligent study of the contributions which they have severally made to the English language, as bequeathed to us jointly by them both. Supposing all other records to have perished, we might still work out and almost reconstitute the history by these aids; even as now, when so many documents, so many institutions survive, this must still be accounted the most important, and that of which the study will introduce us, as no other can, into the innermost heart and life of great periods of our history.

Nor indeed is it hard to see why the language must contain such instruction as this, when we a little realize to ourselves the stages by which it has come down to us in its present shape. There was a time when the languages which the Saxon and the Norman severally spoke, existed each by the side of, but unmingled with the other; one, that of the small dominant class, the other that of the great body of the people. By degrees, however, with the fusion of the two races, the two languages also fused into a third. At once there would exist duplicates for many things. But as in popular speech two words will not long exist side by side to designate the same thing, it became a question how the relative claims of the Saxon and Norman word should adjust themselves, which should remain, which should be dropped; or, if not dropped, should be transferred to some other object, or express some other relation. It is not of course meant that this was ever formally proposed, or as something to be settled by agreement; but practically, one was to be taken, one left. Which was it that should maintain its ground? Evidently where a word was often on the lips of one race, its equivalent seldom on those of the other, where it intimately cohered with the manner of life of one, was only remotely in contact with that of the other, where it laid strong hold on one, but slight on the other, the issue could not be doubtful. In several cases the matter was simpler still: it was not that one word expelled the other, or that rival claims had to be adjusted; but there never had existed more than one word, the thing having been quite strange to the other section of the nation.

Here is the explanation of the assertion just now made—namely, that we might almost reconstruct our history, so far as it turned upon the Norman conquest, by an analysis of our present language, a mustering of its words in groups, and a close observation of the nature and character of those which the two races have severally contributed to it. Thus we should confidently conclude that the Norman was the ruling race, from the noticeable fact that all the words of dignity, state, honor, and pre-eminence, with one remarkable exception (to be adduced presently), descend to us from them—sovereign, sceptre, throne, realm, royalty, homage, prince, duke, count, ("earl" indeed is Scandinavian, though he must borrow his "countess" from the Norman), chancellor, treasurer, palace, castle, hall, dome, and a multitude more. At the same time the one remarkable exception of "king" would make us, even did we know nothing of the actual facts, suspect that the chieftain of this ruling race came in not upon a new title, not as overthrowing a former dynasty, but claiming to be in the rightful line of its succession; that the true continuity of the nation had not, in fact any more than in word, been entirely broken, but survived, in due time to assert itself anew.

And yet, while the statelier superstructure of the language, almost all articles of luxury, all that has to do with the chase, with chivalry, with personal adornment, is Norman throughout; with the broad basis of the language, and therefore of the life, it is otherwise. The great features of nature, sun, moon, and stars, earth, water, and fire, all the prime social relations, father, mother, husband, wife, son, daughter, these are Saxon. The palace and the castle may have come to us from the Norman, but to the Saxon we owe far dearer names, the house, the roof, the home, the hearth. His "board" too, and often probably it was no more, has a more hospitable sound than the "table" of his lord. His sturdy arms turns the soil; he is the boor, the hind, the churl; or if his Norman master has a name for him, it is one which on his lips becomes more and more a title of opprobrium and contempt, the villain. The instruments used in cultivating the earth, the flail, the plough, the sickle, the spade, are expressed in his language; so too the main products, of the earth, as wheat, rye, oats, bere, i. e. barley; and no less the names of domestic animals. Concerning these last it is not a little characteristic to observe (and it may be remembered that Wamba, the Saxon jester in *Ivanhoe*, plays the philologer here), that the names of almost all animals so long as they are alive, are thus Saxon, but when dressed and prepared for food become Norman—a fact indeed which we might have expected beforehand; for the Saxon hind had the charge and labor of tending and feeding them, but only that they might appear on the table of his Norman lord. Thus ox, steer, cow, are Saxon, but beef Norman; calf is Saxon, but veal Norman; sheep is Saxon, but mutton Norman; so it is severally with swine and pork, deer and venison, fowl and pullet. Bacon, the only flesh which perhaps ever came within his reach is the single exception.

Putting all this together, with much more of the same kind, which might be produced, but has only been indicated here, we should certainly gather, that while there are manifest tokens as preserved in our language, of the Saxon having been for a season an inferior and even an oppressed race, the stable elements of Anglo-Saxon life, however overlaid for a while, had still made good their claim to be the solid groundwork of the after nation as of the after language; and to the justice of this conclusion all other historic records, and the present social condition of England, consent in bearing testimony.

What I have here supposed might be done in the way of reproducing the past history of England, had all records of her earlier times, and of the great social changes of those times, been entirely swept away, this has been done for the earlier history of Italy, of which the written memorials *have* thus perished, by a great modern historian of Rome. He draws most important conclusions respecting the races which occupied the Italian soil, and the relations in which they stood to one another, from an analysis of the words which in the Latin language are derived severally from a Greek and from other sources. "It can not," he says, "be mere chance that the words for house, field, plough, ploughing, wine, oil, milk, kine, swine, and others relating to tillage and gentler ways of life agree in Latin and in Greek, while all objects appertaining to war or the chase are designated by words utterly un-Grecian." Hence, he draws the conclusion that this un-Grecian population which has bequeathed these latter words stood toward the Grecian very much in the same relation which we have seen the Norman, as declared by the consenting witness of history and language, to have occupied in respect of the Saxon.

Thus far our lesson has been derived from a noting of the relative proportions in which the words of one stock and of another are mingled in a language, with the domains of human activity to which these severally appertain. But this is not all; there are vast harvests of historic lore garnered often in single words; there are continually great facts of history which they at once declare and preserve. Thus, for instance, is it with the word "church." There can,

I think, be no reasonable doubt that "church" is originally from the Greek, and signifies, "that which pertains to the Lord," or "the house which is the Lord's." But here a difficulty meets us. How explain the presence of a Greek word in the vocabulary of our Anglo-Saxon forefathers? for that *we* derive the word mediately from them, and not immediately from the Greek, is certain. What contact, direct or indirect, was there between the languages to account for this? The explanation is curious. While the Anglo-Saxons and other tribes of the Teutonic stock were *almost* universally converted by their contact with the Latin church in the western provinces of the Roman empire, or by its missionaries, yet it came to pass that before this, some of the Goths on the lower Danube had been brought to the knowledge of Christ by Greek missionaries from Constantinople; and this word κυριακή or "church" did, with certain others, pass over from the Greek to the Gothic tongue; and these Goths, the first converted to the Christian faith, the first, therefore, that had a Christian vocabulary, lent the word in their turn to the other German tribes, among others to our Anglo-Saxon forefathers; thus it has come round by the Goths from Constantinople to us.*

* The passage most illustrative of the parentage of the word is from Walafrid Strabo (about 840) who writes thus: "Ab ipsis autem Græcis Kyrch à Kyrios — et alia multa accepimus. Sicut domus Dei Basilica, i. e., Regia à Rege, sic etiam Kyrica, i. e., Dominica à Domino nuncupatur. Si autem quæritur, quâ occasione ad nos ves-

Or, again, examine the words "pagan" and "paganism," and you will find that there is history in them. Many of us no doubt are aware that the word "pagani," derived from "pagus," a village, signifies properly the dwellers in hamlets and villages, as distinguished from the inhabitants of towns and cities; and the word was so used, and without any religious significance, in the earlier periods of the Latin language. "Pagani" did indeed then not unfrequently designate *all* civilians, as contradistinguished from the military caste; and this fact may not have been without its influence, when the idea of the faithful as soldiers of Christ was strongly realized in the minds of men. But how mainly was it that it came first to be employed as equivalent to "heathen," and applied to those yet alien from the faith of Christ? It was in this way: The Christian church fixed itself first in the seats and centres of intelligence, in the towns and cities of the Roman empire, and in them its first triumphs were won; while long after these had accepted the truth, heathen superstitions and idolatries languished and lingered on in the obscure hamlets and villages of the country; so that "pagans," or villagers, came to be applied to all the remaining votaries of the old and decaying superstitions, inasmuch as far the

tigia hæc græcitatis advenerint, dicendum præcipuè à Gothis, qui et Getæ, cum eo tempore, quo ad fidem Christi perducti sunt, in Græcorum provinciis commorantes, nostrum, i. e., theotiscum sermonem habuerint."

greater number of them were of this class. The first document in which the word appears in this its secondary sense is an edict of the emperor Valentinian, of date A. D. 368. The word "heathen" acquired its meaning from exactly the same fact, namely, that at the introduction of Christianity into Germany, the wild dwellers on the "heaths" longest resisted the truth. Here, then, are two instructive notices for us—first, the historic fact that the church of Christ did thus plant itself first in the haunts of learning and intelligence; and then the more important moral fact, that it shunned not discussion, that it feared not to grapple with the wit and wisdom of this world, or to expose its claims to the searching examination of educated men; but, on the contrary, had its claims first recognised by them, and in the great cities of the world won first a complete triumph over all opposing powers.*

I quoted the words of one in my first lecture, who, magnifying the advantage of following up the history of a word, observed that oftentimes more would be learned from this than from the history of a campaign.† On the strength of this assertion let us take

* There is an interesting and learned note upon the word "pagan" in Gibbon's *Decline and Fall*, c. 21, at the end; and in Grimm's *Deutsche Mythol.*, p. 1198; and the history of the changes in the word's meaning is traced in another interest in Mill's *Logic*, v. 2, p. 271.

† Let me mention here, as I shall not follow them out in this volume, which is rather suggestive than anything else, the following

the word "sacrament," and see whether its history, while it carries us far, yet will not carry us by ways full of instruction; and this, while we seek to trace out merely and strictly the world's history, not needlessly mixing ourselves with discussions in regard of the thing, or of its place and importance in the Christian scheme. We shall find ourselves first among the forms of Roman law, where the "sacramentum" first appears, as the deposite or pledge which in certain suits plaintiff and defendant were alike bound to make, and whereby they engaged themselves to one another, the loser of the suit forfeiting his pledge to sacred temple-uses, from which fact the name "sacramentum," or thing consecrated, was derived. The next employment of the word would plant us amid the military affairs of Rome, "sacramentum" being applied to the military oath with which the Roman soldiers mutually engaged themselves at their first enlisting never to desert their standards, or turn their back upon the enemy, or abandon their imperator—this use of the word teaching us the sacredness which the Romans attached to their military engagements, and going far to explain to us their victories. The word was then transferred from this military oath to any solemn oath whatsoever.

This, which has hitherto been traced, we may call the history of the word, anterior to the period when

words, "sophist," "barbarous," "clerk," "romance," of which it seems to me eminently true that they have such a history as this.

it was assumed into Christian usage at all, and these three stages it had already passed through, before the church claimed it for her own, before indeed she had herself come into existence. Her early writers, out of a sense of the sacredness and solemnity of the oath among all human transactions, first used the word to signify any sacred transaction whatsoever that had some special solemnity or sanctity attached to it, and especially any mystery where more was meant than met the eye or the ear. Thus in the early church writers the Incarnation is a "sacrament," the lifting up of the brazen serpent is a "sacrament," the giving of the manna, and many things more. This period of the word's history it is very expedient that we be aware of, and acquainted with it; for thus all force is taken away from the passages quoted by Romish controversialists in proof of their seven sacraments. It is quite true that the early church writers did entitle marriage, and supreme unction, and the others which they have added, "sacraments;" but then they called "sacraments" or mysteries many things more, which even the theologians of Rome themselves do not pretend to include in the "sacraments" properly so called; so that the evidence here is unfortunately too good; proving too much, it proves nothing. But there is another stage in the word's history, and that stage the one which concerns us the most nearly of all, its limitation to the two "sacraments," properly so called, of the Christian church. The remembrance of the use of "sacrament," a use which had not passed away, to signify the plighted troth of the Roman soldier to his imperator, was that, I think, which specially wrought to the adaptation of the word to baptism; wherein we also, with a manifest allusion to this oath of theirs, pledge ourselves "to fight manfully under Christ's banner, and to continue his faithful soldiers and servants to our life's end;" while the *mysterious* character of the holy Eucharist was, I believe, its especial point of fitness for having this name of "sacrament" applied to it.

I have already sought to find history embedded in the word "frank;" but I must bring forward the Franks again, and ask you to consider whether the well-known fact that in the East not Frenchmen alone, but *all* Europeans are so called, does not require to be accounted for? It can be so, and this wide usage of the word is indeed a deep foot-print of the past. This appellation dates from the Crusades, and Michaud, the chief French historian of these, finds herein, and I think with justice, an evidence that the French took a decided lead, as their gallantry well fitted them to do, in these great romantic enterprises of the middle ages; impressed themselves so strongly on the mind and imagination of the East as *the* crusading nation of Europe, that their name was extended to all the warriors of the West. And remembering how large a proportion of the noblest Crusaders, as well as of others most influential in bringing them about, as Peter the Hermit, Urban the Second, St. Bernard, were French, it must be allowed that the actual facts bear him out in his assertion.

To the Crusades also, probably, and to the intense hatred which they roused throughout Christendom against the Mahometan infidels, we owe "miscreant," in its present sense of one to whom we would attribute the vilest principles and practice. It meant at the first simply a "misbeliever," and would have been used as freely and with as little sense of injustice, of the royal-hearted Saladin as of the most infamous wretch that fought in his armies. By degrees, however, those who employed it put more and more of their feeling and passion into it, and ever lost sight more of its etymology, until they would apply it to any whom they regarded with feelings of abhorrence resembling those which they entertained for an infidel; just as "Samaritan" was often employed by the Jews purely as a term of reproach, and with no thought whether the person on whom it was fastened was really sprung from that mongrel people or not; indeed where they were quite sure that he was not. The word "assassin," also, the explanation of which however we must be content to leave, belongs probably to a romantic chapter in the history of the Crusades.*

* Gibbon's *Decline and Fall*, c. 64.

Once more, the words "saunter" and "saunterer" are singular records of the same events. "Saunterer," derived from "la Sainte Terre," is one who visits the Holy Land. At first a deep and earnest enthusiasm drew men thither to visit—in the beautiful words which Shakespere puts into the mouth of our Fourth Henry, and which explain so well the attractions that at one time made Palestine the magnet of all Christendom—to visit, I say—

> "those holy fields,
> Over whose acres walked those blessèd feet,
> Which fourteen hundred years ago were nailed
> For our advantage on the bitter cross."

By degrees, however, as the enthusiasm spent itself, the making of this pilgrimage degenerated into a mere worldly fashion, and every idler that liked strolling about better than performing the duties of his calling, assumed the pilgrim's staff, and proclaimed himself bound for the Holy Land; to which very often he never in earnest set out. And thus this word forfeited the more honorable meaning it may once have possessed, and the "saunterer" came to signify one idly and unprofitably wasting his time, loitering here and there, with no fixed purpose or aim.

A curious piece of history is wrapped up in the word "poltroon," supposing it to be indeed derived, as many excellent etymologists have considered, from the Latin "pollice truncus;" one, that is deprived, or who has deprived himself, of his thumb. We know that in the old times a self-mutilation of this description was not unfrequent on the part of some cowardly shirking fellow, who wished to escape his share in the defence of his country; he would cut off his right thumb, and at once become incapable of drawing the bow, and thus useless for the wars. It was not to be wondered at that Englishmen, the men of Crecy and Agincourt, who with those very bows which he had disabled himself from drawing, had quelled the mailed chivalry of Europe, should have looked with extremest disdain on one who had so basely exempted himself from service, nor that the "pollice truncus," the poltroon, first applied to a coward of this sort, should afterward become a name of scorn affixed to every base and cowardly evader of the duties and dangers of life.* Our use of the word "caitiff," which is identical with "captive," only coming through the Norman French, has, in like manner, its rise out of the sense that he who lets himself be made prisoner in war is a worthless, good-for-nothing person — a feeling so

* See *The Diversions of Purley*, part ii., chap. 2. — In Bonaparte's wars exactly the same thing happened, and young men cut off not now the thumb, but the forefinger, that which should pull the trigger, so to escape being drawn for the conscription; and travellers in Egypt tell us that under the horrible tyranny of Mehemet Ali, a great part of the population in some of the villages had deprived themselves of the sight of the right eye, that in like manner they might be useless for war.

strong in some states of antiquity, that under no circumstances would they consent to ransom those of their citizens who had fallen alive into the hands of the enemy. The captives were accounted "caitiffs," whom they could better do without. The same feeling has given us "craven," a synonym for coward: this is one who has *craved* or *craven* his life at the enemies' hands, instead of resisting to the death.

Various derivations of "cardinal" have been proposed; or, to speak more accurately, it has been sought in various ways to account for the appropriating of this name to the parochial clergy of the city of Rome with the subordinate bishops of the diocese. I believe the application of the name is an outgrowth, and itself a standing testimony, of the measureless assumptions of the Romish see. One of the favorite comparisons by which that see sought to set out its relation of superiority to all the other churches of Christendom was this: it was the "hinge" or "cardo" on which all the rest of the church, as the door, at once depended and turned. It followed presently upon this that the clergy of Rome were "cardinales," as nearest and most closely connected with him who was thus the "hinge" or "cardo" of all.*

* Thus a letter, professing to be one of Pope Anacletus the First in the first century, but really forged in the ninth: "Apostolica Sedes *cardo* et caput omnium Ecclesiarum à Domino est constituta; et sicut cardine ostium regitur, sic hujus S. Sedis auctoritate omnes Ecclesiæ reguntur." And we have "cardinal" put in relation with this "cardo" in a genuine letter of Pope Leo the Ninth: "Clerici summæ Sedis *Cardinales* dicuntur, *cardini* utique illi quo cætera moventur, vicinius adhærentes."

There is a little word not in uncommon use among us, an inquiry into the pedigree of which will lay open to us an important page in the intellectual history of the world. We may all know what a "dunce" is, but we may not be as well acquainted with the quarter whence the word has been derived. Certain theologians in the middle ages were termed schoolmen; being so called because they were formed in the cloister and cathedral schools which Charlemagne had founded — men not to be lightly spoken of, as now they often are by those who never read a line of their works, and have not a tithe of their wit; who moreover little guess how many of the most familiar words which they employ, or misemploy, have descended to them from these. "Real," "virtual," "entity," "nonentity," "equivocation," all these, with many more unknown to classical Latin, but which now have become almost necessities, were first coined by the schoolmen, and passing over from them into the language of those more or less interested in their speculations, have gradually filtered through the successive strata of society, till now they have reached, some of them, to quite the lowest. At the revival of learning, however, their works fell out of favor: they were not written in classical Latin: the form in which their speculations were thrown was often unattractive; it was mainly in their authority that the Romish church found support for many of its periled dogmas; on all which accounts, it was considered a mark of intellectual progress and advance to have broken with them and altogether thrown off their yoke. Some, however, still clung to these Schoolmen, and to one in particular, *Duns* Scotus, the great teacher of the Franciscan order; and many times an adherent of the old learning would seek to strengthen his position by an appeal to its great doctor, familiarly called Duns; while the others would contemptuously rejoin, "Oh, you are a *Dunsman*," or more briefly, "You are a *Duns*"—or, "This is a piece of *dunsery*;" and inasmuch as the new learning was ever enlisting more and more of the genius and scholarship of the age on its side, the title became more and more a term of scorn: "Remember ye not," says Tyndal, "how within this thirty years and far less, the old barking curs, *Dunce's* disciples, and like draff called Scotists, the children of darkness, raged in every pulpit against Greek, Latin, and Hebrew?" And thus from that long extinct conflict between the old and the new learning, that strife between the mediæval and the modern theology, we inherit the words, "dunce," and "duncery." Let us pause here for a moment to confess that the lot of poor Duns was certainly a hard one, who, whatever may have been his merits as a teacher of Christian truth, was certainly one of the keenest and most subtle-witted of men. He, the "subtle doctor" by pre-eminence, for so his admirers called him, could hardly have anticipated, and as little as any man deserved, that his name should be turned into a by-word expressive of stupidity and obstinate dullness. This, however, is only one example of the curious fortune of words. We have another singular example of the same, and of a parallel injustice, in the way in which the word "mammetry," which is a contraction of "Mahometry," is employed by our early English writers. Mahometanism being the most prominent form of false religion with which Englishmen were acquainted, this word was used up to and beyond the Reformation, to designate first any false religion, and then the worship of idols; idolatry being proper to, and a leading feature of most false religions. They did not pause to remember that Mahometanism is the great exception, its most characteristic feature and glory being its protest against all idol-worship whatsoever; which being so, the injustice was signal in calling an idol a "mammet" or a Mahomet, and idolatry, "mammetry." To pursue the fortunes of the word a little further, another step caused not religious images only, but dolls to be called "mammets;" and when in *Romeo and Juliet* Capulet contemptuously styles his daughter "a whining *mammet*," the process is strange, yet every step of it may be easily traced, whereby the name of the Arabian false prophet is fastened on the fair maiden of Verona.

Nor is the true derivation of "tariff" unworthy to

be traced. We all know what it means, namely, a fixed scale of duties, levied upon imports. If you turn to a map of Spain, you will take note at its southern point, and running out into the straits of Gibraltar, of a promontory, which from its position is admirably adapted for commanding the entrance of the Mediterranean sea, and watching the exit and entrance of all ships. A fortress stands upon this promontory, called now, as it was also called in the times of the Moorish domination in Spain, "Tarifa;" the name indeed is of Moorish origin. It was the custom of the Moors to watch from this point all merchant-ships going into, or coming out of, the Mid-land sea; and issuing from this stronghold, to levy duties according to a fixed scale on all merchandise passing in and out of the straits, and this was called from the place where it was levied, "tarifa" or "tariff;" and in this way we have acquired the word.

"Bigot" is another word widely spread over Europe, of which I am inclined to think that we should look for the derivation where it is not generally sought, and that here too we must turn to Spain for the explanation. It has much perplexed inquirers, and two explanations of it are current; one of which traces it up to the early Normans, while they yet retained their northern tongue, and to their often abjuration by the name of God, with sometimes reference to a famous scene in French history in which Rollo, duke of Normandy, played a conspicuous part; the other puts it in connection with "beguines," called often in Latin "beguttæ," a name by which certain communities of pietist women were known in the middle ages. Yet I can not but think it probable that rather than to either of these sources we owe the word to that mighty impression which the Spaniards began to make upon all Europe in the fifteenth century, and made for a long time after. Now the word "bigote," means in Spanish "mustachio;" and as contrasted with the smooth or nearly smooth upper lip of most other people, at that time the Spaniards were the "men of the mustachio." That it was their characteristic feature comes out in Shakspere's *Love's Labor's Lost*, where Armado, the "fantastical Spaniard," describes the king "his familiar, as sometimes being pleased to lean on his poor shoulder, and dally with his mustachio."* That they themselves connected firmness and resolution with the mustachio, that it was esteemed the outward symbol of these, is plain from such phrases as "hombre de bigote," a man of resolution, "tener bigotes," to stand firm. But that in which they eminently displayed their firmness and resolution in those days was their adherence to whatever the Roman see required and taught. What then more natural, or more entirely according to the law of the generation of names, than that this striking and distinguishing outward feature of the Spaniard should have been laid hold of to ex-

Act 5 sc. 1.

press that character and condition which eminently were his, and then transferred to all others who shared the same? The mustachio is in like manner in France a symbol of military courage; and thus "un vieux moustache" is an old soldier of courage and military bearing. And strengthening this view, the earliest use of the word which Richardson gives, is a passage from Bishop Hall, where "bigot" is used to signify a pervert to Romanism: "he was turned both *bigot* and physician." In further proof that the Spaniard was in those times the standing representative of the bigot and the persecutor, we need but turn to the older editions of Fox's *Book of Martyrs*, where the pagan persecutors of the early Christians are usually arrayed in the armor of Spanish soldiers, and sometimes graced with tremendous "bigotes."

Having dedicated this lecture to the history which is in words. I can have no fitter opportunity of urging upon you the importance of seeking in every case to acquaint yourselves with the circumstances under which any body of men, that have played an important part in history, especially in the history of your own land, obtained the name by which they were afterward willing to be known, or which was used for their designation by others. This you may do as a matter of historical inquiry, and keeping entirely aloof in spirit from the scorn, the bitterness, the falsehood the calumny, out of which very often this name was first imposed. Whatever of this evil may have been at work in them that coined, or gave currency to, the name, the name itself can never be neglected without serious loss by those who would truly understand the moral significance of the thing; there is always something, often very much, to be learned from it. Learn then in regard of each one of these names which you may meet in your studies, whether it was one which men gave to themselves; or one imposed on them by others, and which they never recognised; or one which being first imposed by others, was yet in course of time admitted and accepted by themselves. We have examples in all these kinds. Thus the "gnostics" called *themselves* such; the name was of their own devising, and one in which they boasted: in like manner the "cavaliers" of our civil war.* "Quaker," "puritan," "roundhead," were all, on the contrary, names devised by others, and never accepted by them to whom they were attached; while "whig" and "tory" were nicknames originally indeed of bitterest scorn and party hate, given by two political bodies in England to one another,† which, however, in course of years lost what was offensive in them, until they came to be accepted and employed by the very parties themselves. The same we may say of "methodist;" it was certainly not first taken by the followers of Wesley, but im-

* See Roger North's *Examen.*, p. 321, for a very lively, though not a very impartial account, of the rise of these names.

† See Clarendon's *History of the Rebellion*, b. 4.

posed on them by others, while yet they have been subsequently willing to accept and to be known by it.

Now of these titles, and of many more that might be adduced, some undoubtedly had their rise in mere external accident, and stand in no essential connection with those that bear them; and these, although not without their instruction, yet plainly are not so instructive as other names, in which the innermost heart of a system speaks out and reveals itself, so that, having mastered the name, we have placed ourselves at the central point, and that from which we shall best master everything besides. Thus for instance is it with "gnosticism" and "gnostic;" in the prominence given to *gnosis*, or knowledge, as opposed to faith, lies the key to the whole system. And I may say generally that almost all the sects and parties, religious and political, which have risen up in times past in England, are known by names that will repay study; an entering into which will bring us far in the understanding of their strength and their weakness, their truth and their error, the idea and intention according to which they wrought. "Puritans," "fifth-monarchy men," "seekers," "independents," "friends," "latitudinarians," these titles with many more have each its significance; and would you understand what *they* meant, you must first understand what they were called. From this must be your point of starting, even as to this you must bring back whatever later information you may gain;

5

and, though I will not say that you must always subordinate it to the name, yet must you ever put it in relation and connection with that.

You will often be able to glean knowledge from the names of things, if not as important as that I have just been speaking of, yet curious and interesting. What a record of invention is presented in the names which so many articles bear, of the place from which they first came, or the person by whom they were first invented. The "bayonet" tells us that it was first made at Bayonne—"cambrics" that they came from Cambray—"damask" from Damascus—"arras" from the city of the same name—"cordwain" or "cordova" from Cordova—"currants" from Corinth—the "guinea," that it was originally coined of gold brought from the African coast so called—"camlet" that it was woven, at least in part, of camel's hair. Such has been the manufacturing progress of England that we now send our calicoes and muslins to India and the east; yet the words give standing witness that we once imported them thence; for "calico" is from Calicut, and "muslin" from Moussul, a city in Asiatic Turkey.

It is true indeed that occasionally names embody and give permanence to an error; as when in the name "America" the honor of discovering the New World, which belonged to Columbus, has been transferred to another eminent discoverer, but to one who had no title to this praise, and who did not, as has been lately abundantly shown, by any means desire to claim it for himself. So, too, the "turkey" in our farm-yards seems to claim Turkey for its home; and the assumption that it was thence no doubt caused it to be so called; while indeed it was unknown in Europe until introduced from the New World, where alone it is indigenous. This error the French in another shape repeat, calling it "dinde," which was originally "poulet *d'Inde*," or, Indian fowl. In like manner "gypsies" appears to imply that Egypt was the country to which these wanderers originally belonged, and from which they had migrated westward; and certainly it was so believed in many parts of Europe at their first appearance in the beginning of the fifteenth century, and hence this title. It is now however clearly made out, their language leaving no doubt of the fact, that they are an outcast tribe, which has wandered hither from a more distant land, from India itself. "Bohemians," which is the French appellation of gypsies, involves an error similar to ours. They were taken at first by the common people in France to be the expelled Hussites of Bohemia, and hence this name. In the German "zigeuner" there is no expression of the land from which they were assumed to have come, but if this word be "zieh-gauner," roaming thieves, it will then indicate the evil repute in which from the very beginning they were held.

And where words have not, as in these cases, embodied an error, it will yet sometimes happen that the sound or spelling of a word will to *us* possibly suggest a wrong explanation, against which in these studies it will need to be on our guard. I dare say that there has been a stage in most boys' geographical knowledge, when they have taken for granted that Jutland was so called, not because it was the land of the Jutes, but on account of its *jutting* out into the sea in so remarkable a manner. And there have not been wanting those who have ventured to trace in the name "Jove" a heathen reminiscence of the awful name of Jehovah. I will not enter into this here; sufficient to say that, however specious this at first sight may seem, yet on closer examination of the two words, every connection between them disappears.

Sometimes the assumed derivation has reacted upon and modified the spelling. Thus the name of the Caledonian tribe whom we call the "Picts," would probably have come down to us in a somewhat different form, but for the assumption which early rose up, that they were so called from their custom of staining or painting their bodies, that in fact "Picts" meant "the painted." This, as is now acknowledged, is an exceedingly improbable supposition. It would be quite conceivable that the Romans should have given this name to the *first* barbarous tribe they encountered, who were in the habit of painting themselves thus; such a custom, forcing itself on the eye, and impressing itself on the imagination, is exactly that which gives birth to a name: but after they had been long familiar with the tribes in southern Britain, to whom this painting or tattooing was equally familiar, it is quite inconceivable that they should have applied it to one of the northern tribes in the island, with which they first came in contact at a far later day. The name is much more probably the original Celtic one belonging to the tribe, slightly altered in the mouths of the Romans.—It may have been the same with "hurricane;" for many have imagined that this word, being used especially to signify the West Indian tornado, must be derived from the tearing up and *hurrying* away of the *canes* in the sugar plantations, just in the same way as the Latin "calamitas" has been drawn, but erroneously, from "calamus," the stalk of the corn. In both cases the etymology is faulty; "hurricane" is only a transplanting into our tongue of the Spanish "hurracan" or the French "ouragan."*

* One or two words more I will mention here, in which a falsely imagined etymology has certainly gone so far as often, if not always, to influence the spelling. How could the *h*, for example, have ever found its way into "posthumous," but for the erroneous assumption that it had something to do with *post humum*, instead of being the superlative of "posterus"? "Surname," too, is spelled by many with an *i*, as if it were "sire"-name, the family name in contradistinction to the personal or Christian, when indeed it is the name over and above ("sur" for "super"), as I shall have occasion to note in a later lecture. "Shame*faced*," too, was once "shame*fast*," "shame*faced*ness was "shame*fast*ness," like "stead*fast*" and "stead*fast*ness:" but

It is a signal evidence of the conservative powers of language, that we may oftentimes trace in speech the records of customs and states of society which have now passed so entirely away as to survive nowhere else but in these words alone. For example, a "stipulation," or agreement, is so called, as many are strong to affirm, from "stipula," a straw, because it once was usual, when one person passed over landed property to another, that a straw from the land, as a pledge or representative of the property transferred, should be handed from the seller to the buyer, which afterward was commonly preserved with, or inserted in the title-deeds. And we all know how important a fact of English history is laid up in "curfew" or "couvre-feu." Nor need I do more than remind you that in our common phrase of "signing our name," we preserve a record of a time when the first rudiments of education, such as the power of writing, were the portion of so few, that it was not as now the exception, but the custom for most persons to make their mark or "sign," great barons and kings themselves not being ashamed to set this sign or cross to the weightiest documents.

the ordinary manifestations of shame being by the face, have brought it to its present orthography; it was 'shame*fast*ness" at 1 Tim. ii. 9, in the first edition (1611) of the authorized version, and certainly ought not to have been altered. In Latin the same has occurred with "orichalcum," spelled often "aurichalcum," as though it were a composite metal of mingled gold and brass. It is indeed the *mountain* brass, ὀρείχαλκος.

The more accurate language by which to express what now we do, would be to speak of "subscribing the name." Then, too, whenever we speak of arithmetic as the science of "calculation," we in fact allude to that rudimental period of the science of numbers, when pebbles (calculi) were used, as now among savages they often are, to facilitate the practice of counting. In "library" we preserve a record of the fact that books were once written on the bark (liber) of trees, as in "paper," of a somewhat later period, when the Egyptian papyrus, "the paper reeds by the brooks," furnished the chief material employed in writing.

Theories, too, which long since were utterly renounced, have yet left their traces behind them. Thus the words "good humor," "bad humor," "humorous," and the like, rest altogether on a now-exploded, but a very old and widely-extended theory of medicine; according to which there were four principal moistures or "humors" in the natural body, on the due proportion and combination of which the disposition alike of body and of mind depended.* And "temper," as used by us now, has its origin in the same theory; the due admixture, or right "tempering," of these gave what was called the happy "temper," which, thus existing inwardly, manifested itself also outwardly. In the same manner "distemper," which we still employ in the sense

* See the *Prologue* to Ben Jonson's *Every Man out of his Humor.*

of sickness, was that evil frame either of a man's body or of his mind (for it was used alike of both), which had its rise in an unsuitable mingling of these humors. In these instances, as in many more, the great streams of thought and feeling have changed their course, and now flow in quite other channels from those which once they filled, but have left these words as lasting memorials of the channels in which once they ran.

Other singular examples we have of the way in which the record of old errors, themselves exploded long ago, may yet survive in language — the words that grew into use when those errors found credit, maintaining still their currency among us. The mythology, for example, which our ancestors brought with them from the forests of Germany is as much extinct for us as are the Lares, Larvæ, and Lemures of heathen Rome; yet the deposite it has permanently left in the language is not inconsiderable. "Lubber," "dwarf," "oaf," "droll," "hag," "nightmare," suggest themselves at once, as belonging to the old Teutonic demonology. Thus, too, no one now believes in astrology, that the planet under which a man may happen to be born will affect his temperament, will make him for life of a disposition grave or gay, lively or severe. Yet we seem to affirm as much in language, for we speak of a person as "jovial," or "saturnine," or "mercurial" — "jovial," as being born under the planet Jupiter or Jove, which was the joyfullest star, and of the happiest augury of all: a gloomy, severe person is said to be "staurnine," as born under the planet Saturn, who was considered to make those that owned his influence, and were born when he was in the ascendant, grave and stern as himself; another we call "mercurial," that is light-hearted, as those born under the planet Mercury were accounted to be. The same faith in the influence of the stars survives, so far at least as words go, in "disaster," "disastrous," "ill-starred," "ascendant," "ascendency," and, indeed, in the word "influence" itself. What curious legends belong to the explanation of the "*sardonic* laugh;" to the "topaz," so called, as some said, because men were only able to conjecture (τοπάζειν) the place whence it was brought, and to innumerable other of the words employed by us still.

But here a question presents itself, one which might at first sight seem merely speculative, yet which is not altogether so; for it has before now become a veritable case of conscience with some whether they ought to use words which originally rested on, and so seem to affirm, some superstition or untruth. This question has practically settled itself; they will keep their ground; but they also ought. It is not of necessity that a word should always be considered to root itself in its etymology, and to draw its life-blood thence. It may so detach itself from this as to have a right to be regarded independently of it: and thus our weekly newspapers commit no absurdity in calling themselves "journals;" we involve ourselves in no real contradiction, speaking of a "quarantine" of five, ten, or any number of days more or fewer than forty. Thus, too, I remember once asking a class of children in a school, whether an announcement which during one very hard winter appeared in the papers, of a "*white blackbird*" having been shot, was correctly worded, or self-contradictory and absurd. The less thoughtful members of the class instantly pronounced against it; while after some little consideration, some two or three perceived and replied that it was perfectly correct, that while no doubt the bird had originally obtained this name from its blackness, yet was it now the name of a species, and a name which so cleaved to it, as not to be forfeited even when the blackness had ceased altogether to exist. We do not question the right of the "*New* Forest" still to be so called, though it has now stood for nigh eight hundred years.

It must then be esteemed a piece of ethical prudery, and an ignorance of the laws which govern words and their uses, in the early quakers, when they refused to employ the names commonly given to the days of the week, and substituted for these "first day," "second day," and so on; which they did, as is well known, on the ground that it became not Christian men to give so much sanction to idolatry as was involved in the ordinary style — as though every time they spoke of Wednesday they would be doing some honor to Woden, of Thursday to Thor, of Friday to Freya, and thus with the rest. But these names of the days of the week had long left their etymologies behind, and quite disengaged themselves from them. Moreover, had these precisians in speech been consistent, they could not have stopped where they did; every new acquaintance with the derivation or primary use of words would have entangled them in new embarrassment, would have required them still further to purge their vocabulary. "To charm," "to bewitch," "to fascinate," "to enchant," would have been no longer lawful words for those who had outlived the belief in magic, and in the power of the evil eye; nor "lunacy," nor "lunatic," for such as did not believe that the moon had anything to do with mental unsoundness. Nay, they must have found fault with the language of Holy Scripture itself; for in the New Testament there is a word in very honorable use expressing a function that might be exercised by the faithful, that, namely, of an interpreter, which word is yet directly derived from Hermes, a heathen deity, and a deity, who did not, like Woden, Thor, and Freya, pertain to a long extinct mythology, but to one existing at that very moment in its strength. And how was it, we may ask, that Paul did not protest against a Christian woman retaining the name of Phœbe (Rom. xvi. 1), a goddess of the same mythology?

That which has been spoken in this lecture will, I trust, abundantly justify the comparison with which I would conclude it. Suppose, then, that the pieces of money which, in the ordinary intercourse of life, are passing through our hands, had each one something of its own which made it more or less worthy of note; if on one was stamped some striking maxim, on another some important fact, on a third a memorable date; if others were works of finest art, graven with rare and beautiful devices, or bearing the head of some ancient sage or heroic king; while others again were the sole surviving monuments of mighty nations that once filled the world with their fame; what a careless indifference to our own improvement would it argue in us, if we were content that these should come and go, should stay by us or pass from us, without our vouchsafing to them so much as one serious regard. Such a currency there is, a currency intellectual and spiritual of no meaner worth, and one with which we have to transact so much of the higher business of our lives. Let us see that we come not here under the condemnation of any such incurious dullness as that which I have imagined.

LECTURE IV.

THE RISE OF NEW WORDS.

One of the most interesting branches of the study which is occupying us now is the taking note of the periods when great and and significant words, or, it may be, even such as can hardly claim those epithets, have risen up and come into use, with the circumstances attending their rise. The different portions of my theme so run into one another, that this is a subject which I have, though unwillingly, already anticipated in part; yet is it one so curious, and which, I believe, may be made so instructive, that I purpose to dedicate a lecture exclusively to it. Indeed, I am persuaded that a little volume might be constructed, which few of its size would rival in interest, that should do no more than indicate, or, where advisable, give a quotation from, the first writer or the first document in which new words, or old words employed in a new sense—such, I mean, as have afterward played a more or less important part in the world's history—have appeared. For the feeling wherewith one watches the rise above the horizon of these words, some of them to shine for ever as luminaries in the moral and intellectual heaven above us, can oftentimes be only likened to that which the poet so grandly describes, of—

> "some watcher of the skies,
> When a new planet swims into his ken."

I would instance of words religious and ecclesiastical such as these—"Christian,"* "trinity;"† "catholic," as an epithet applied to the church; ‡ "canonical," as a distinctive characteristic of the received Scriptures; § "New Testament," as expressing the complex of the sacred books of the new covenant; ‖ "gospels," as applied to the four inspired records of the life of our Lord; ¶ or again, historical and geographical, as the first mention of India; ** the first emerging of the names "Germany" and the "Germans;" †† the earliest mention of Rome in any writer; ‡‡ or when the entire Hesperian peninsula acquired the title of "Italy," which had been gradually creeping up for centuries from its southern extremity; §§ when Asia on this side

* First in Acts xi. 26.

† First in Tertullian, *Adv. Prax.*, c. 3.

‡ First by Ignatius, *Ad. Smyr.*, c. 8.

§ Origen, *Opp.* v. 3, p. 36. (Ed. de la Rue.)

‖ Tertullian, *Adv. Marc.*, iv. 1; *Adv. Prax.*, 15, 20.

¶ Justin Martyr, *Apol.* i. 66.

** Æschylus, *Suppl.*, 282.

†† They probably first occur in the writings of Cæsar.

‡‡ Probably in Hellanicus, a contemporary of Herodotus.

§§ In the time of Augustus Cæsar. Merivale (*Hist. of the Rom.*, v. 3. p. 157) notices what he believes the first use of it which has come down to us in this its widest sense.

Taurus was first called "Asia Minor;"* the earliest notice which we have of the "Normans," under this title;"† who first gave to the newly-discovered continent in the west the name of "America," and when; ‡ the period when this island exchanged its earlier name of "Britain" for its new one of "Anglia," or, "England;" or, again, when it resumed "Great Britain," as its official designation; so, too, to go back in the world's history, and to take one or two examples of a different character—at what moment the words "tyrant" and "tyranny," marking so distinct an epoch as they do in the political history of Greece, first appeared; § when and from whom

* The name first occurs in Orosius, i. 2; that is, in the fifth century of our æra.

† In the Geographer of Ravenna.

‡ Alexander von Humboldt, who has studied the question closely, ascribes its general reception to its having been introduced into a popular and influential work on geography, published in 1507.

§ First in the writings of Archilochus, about B. C. 700. I will just observe, that "tyrant," with the Greeks, had a much deeper sense than it has in our modern use. The difference between a king and a tyrant was much more deeply apprehended by them than by us. A tyrant was not a bad king, one who abused the advantages of a rightful position to purposes of lust, or cruelty, or other oppression; but it was of the essence of the tyrant that he attained supreme dominion through a violation of the laws and liberties of the state, and such a one, with whatever moderation he might afterward exercise his rule, would not the less retain the name. Thus, the mild and bounteous Pisistratus was, and was called, "tyrant" of Athens; while a Christian the Second, of Denmark, would not have been esteemed such in their eyes. It was to the honor of the Greeks that they did not allow the course of the word to be arrested or turned aside by any occasional or partial exceptions in the manner of the after-exercise of this ill-gotten dominion, but in the hateful secondary the fabric of the external universe first received the title of "cosmos," or, "beautiful order;"* with many more of the same description.

Of these which I have just adduced let us take, by way of sample, two, and try whether there is not much to be gathered from them, and from attending to the epoch and circumstances of their rise. Our first example is a remarkable one, for it shows us the Holy Spirit himself, counting a name, and the rise of a name of so much importance as to make it matter of special record in the Book of Life. "The disciples were called *Christians* first in Antioch." (Acts xi. 26.) This might seem at first sight a notice curious and interesting, as all must possess interest for us which relates to the early days of the church, but nothing more. And yet in truth how much of history is enfolded in this name; what light it throws on the early history of Christianity to know when and where it was first imposed on the faithful —"imposed," I say, for it is clearly a name which

sense which the word even with them acquired, and which is felt still more strongly by us, the moral conviction, justified by all experience, spake out, that what was gotten by fraud and violence would only by the same methods be retained; that the "tyrant," in the earlier Greek sense of the word, dogged as he would be by suspicion, fear, and an evil conscience, must also by a sure law become a "tyrant" in the later, which is that in which alone we employ the word. The present ruler of France, in the manner in which he got his power, and in the manner in which he wields it, casts the broadest light on the whole history of the word.

* The word is ascribed, as is well known, to Pythagoras, born about B. C. 570.

they did not give to themselves, but received from their adversaries, however afterward they may have learned to accept it as a title of honor, and to glory in it. For it is not said that they "*called themselves*," but "*were called*" Christians first at Antioch; nor do we find the name anywhere in scripture except on the lips of those alien from, or opposed to, the gospel. (Acts xxvi. 28; 1 Pet. iv. 16.) And as it was a name imposed by adversaries, so among those adversaries it was plainly the heathen, and not the Jews, that gave it; since the Jews would never have called the followers of Jesus of Nazareth, "Christians," or "those of Christ," seeing that the very point of their opposition to him was, that he was not the Christ, but a false pretender to this name.

Starting then from this point, that "Christians" was a name given to the early disciples by the heathen, let us see what we may learn from it. Now we know that Antioch was the headquarters of the earliest missions to the heathen, even as Jerusalem was to those of the seed of Abraham. It was there and among the faithful there that the sense of the world-wide destination of the gospel arose; there it was first plainly seen as intended for all kindreds of the earth. Hitherto the faithful in Christ had been called by their enemies, and indeed often were still called, "Galileans," or "Nazarenes"—both names which indicated the Jewish cradle in which the gospel had been nursed, and that the world saw in it no more than a Jewish sect. But the name "Christians," or "those of Christ," imposed upon them now, while it indicated that Christ and the confession of his name was felt even by the world to be the sum and centre of their religion, showed also that the heathen had now come to comprehend, I do not say what the church would be, but what it claimed to be — no mere variety of Judaism, but a society with a world-wide mission; it is clear that, when this name was given, the church, even in the world's eyes, had chipped its Jewish shell. Nor will the attentive reader fail to observe that the imposing of this name on believers is by closest juxtaposition connected in the sacred narrative, and still more closely in the Greek than in the English, with St. Paul's first arrival at Antioch, and preaching there; he being the especial and appointed instrument for bringing the church into the recognition of this its destination for all men. As so often happens with the rise of a new name, the rise of this one marked a new epoch in the church's life, its entrance upon a new stage of its development.

It is a merely subordinate matter, but yet I might just observe how strikingly what we know from other quarters confirms the accuracy of this account, which lays the invention of this name to the credit of the Antiochenes. Antioch, with its idle and witty inhabitants, was famous in all antiquity for the invention of nicknames. It was a manufacture in which they particularly excelled: and thus it was exactly the place, where beforehand we might have expected that such a name, being a nickname or little better in the mouths of those that devised it, should have sprung up.

Our other example shall be "Anglia," or "England." When and under what circumstances did this island exchange for this its earlier name of Britain, which it had borne for more than a thousand years? There seems no sufficient reason for calling in question, though some have so done, the statement of the old chronicler that it received this new name of Anglia from Egbert, king of Wessex, who with the sanction of his parliament or witanegemot, holden A. D. 800 in this very city of Winchester, determined that the name "Britain" should give place to "England." It may be that the change was not effected by any such formal act as this, yet the accuracy of the old historian, so far at least as his date is concerned, receives strong confirmation from the circumstance that "Anglia," which is nowhere to be traced in any documents anterior to this period, does immediately after begin to appear.

What lessons for the student of English history are here, in the knowledge of this one fact, if he will but seek to look at it all round, and consider it in a thoughtful spirit. I have said that the rise of a new name marks often a new epoch in history; certainly it was so in the instance before us. In the first place, as it is the just law of names, that a people should give a name to the land which they possess, not receive one from it, as the Franks make Gaul to be France, do not suffer themselves to become Gauls, so, as regards our own land, it is plain from the coming up of this name that there must have been now a sense in men's minds that its transformation from a land of Britons to a land of Angles was at length completely accomplished, and might therefore justly claim to find its recognition in a word. That the Normans never made a "Norman-land" out of England, as they had out of Neustria, and as the Angles had made an "Angle-land" out of Britain—that they never so supplanted the population or dissolved the social framework of the Angles, as these had done of the Britons—is evident from the fact that there went along with *their* conquest of the land no such substitution of a new name for the old, no such obliteration of the old by the new, as on that prior occupation of the soil had found place.—And then, further, how significant a fact, that the invading German tribes, which had hitherto been content to call themselves according to the different provinces or districts which they occupied, should have now felt that they needed, and out of that need should have given birth to a name common to and including the whole land. Was there not here a sign that the sense of unity, of all making up one corporate body, one nation, was emerging out of the confusion of the preceding period of the heptarchy? We know from other sources that Egbert was the first who united the different kingdoms of the heptarchy under his single sceptre; the first in whom the nation was knit together into one. How instructive to find a name which should be the symbol of unity, coming to the birth at this very moment. In respect, too, of the relations between themselves of the two most important tribes which had settled in this island, the Angles and the Saxons (the Jutes were too few to contend for the honor), it is assuredly a weighty fact that it was the Angles alone, from whom, though numerically inferior, the new appellation was derived. Doubtless, a moral or political predominance of this tribe, probably a political founded on a moral asserted itself in this fact. We are the less inclined to attribute it to accident from the circumstance that in the phrase "Anglo-Saxons" (Angli-Saxones), a term which is no modern invention of convenience as is sometimes erroneously asserted, but is of earlier use even than Anglia, the Angles have again the precedence, and the Saxons only follow.

It will be seen, I think, by these two examples that new words will repay any attention which we may bestow upon them, and upon the conditions under which they emerge. Let us proceed to consider the causes which give them birth, the periods when a language is most fruitful in them, the regions of society from which they usually proceed, with some other interesting phenomena about them.

The cause then which more than any other creates the necessity for these additions to the vocabulary of a language, and calls forth the words which shall supply this necessity, when it is felt, is beyond a question this—namely, that in the appointments of highest Wisdom there are certain cardinal epochs in the world's history, in which, far more than at other times, new moral and spiritual forces begin to work, and to stir society to its central depths. When it is thus with a people, they make claims upon their language, which were never made upon it hitherto. It is required to utter truths, to express ideas, which were strange to it in the time of its first moulding and shaping, and for which therefore the terms sufficient will naturally not be found in it at once—these new thoughts and feelings being larger and deeper than any with which hitherto the speakers of that tongue had been familiar. But when the bed of a river is suddenly required to deliver a far greater volume of waters than till now has been its wont, it is nothing strange if it should surmount its banks, break forth on the right hand and on the left, or even force new channels with something of violence for itself. The most illustrious example of this whereof I have been speaking, would be, of course, the coming in of Christianity, or, to include the anterior dispensation, we may say, of revealed religion into the ancient heathen world, with the consequent necessity under which the great novel truths which were then proclaimed to mankind lay, of clothing themselves in the language of men, in the languages of Greece and Rome — languages which in their previous form might have sufficed, and did suffice, for heathenism, sensuous and finite as it was, but not for the spiritual and infinite of the new dispensation. How often had the new thoughts to weave a new garment for themselves, inasmuch as that which they found ready made was too narrow to wrap themselves withal; the new wine to find new vessels for itself, that both might be preserved, the old vessels being neither sufficiently strong nor expansive to hold it.

Thus, not to speak of mere technical matters which would claim their utterance, how could the Greek language have had a word for "idolatry," so long as the sense of the awful contrast between the worship of the living God and of dead things had not risen up in their minds that spoke it? But when those began to use Greek, and that as the sole utterance of what was in them, men to whom this distinction and contrast was the most earnest and the deepest conviction of their lives, the words "idolatry," "idolater," of necessity appeared. The heathen claimed not for their deities to be "searchers of hearts," disclaimed not for them the being "accepters of persons;" such attributes of power and righteousness entered not into their minds as pertaining to the objects of their worship. The Greek language, therefore, so long as they only employed it, had not the words corresponding. It indeed could not have, as the Jewish Hellenistic Greek could not be without them.

As these difficulties would be felt the most strongly when the thought and feeling which had been at home in the Hebrew, the original language of inspiration, were to be translated into Greek, the same also would reappear, though naturally not to the same extent, when that which had gradually woven for itself in the Greek an adequate attire, again demanded to find garments in the Latin wherein it might be suitably arrayed. A single example will illustrate this better than long disquisitions. There was in the Greek a word for "savior," which, although it had often been degraded to unworthy uses, having been applied not merely to heathen deities, but bestowed as a title of honor on men, and these such as sometimes were rather "destroyers" than "saviors" of their fellows, was yet in itself sufficient to set forth that central office and dignity of Christ —the word being like some profaned temple, which did not need to be rebuilt, but only to be consecrated anew. With the Latin it was otherwise; the language seemed to be without a word of such frequent recurrence, and essential use to Christianity: indeed

Cicero, than whom none could know better the capabilities of his own tongue, distinctly declared that it possessed no single word corresponding to the Greek "savior."* "Salvator" would have been the natural word; but the classical Latin, though it had "salus" and "salvus," had neither this, nor the verb "salvare;" I say the classical, for some believe that "salvare" had always existed in the common speech. "Servator" was instinctively felt to be insufficient, even as in English "preserver" would fall very short of uttering all for us which "savior" does now; the seeking of the strayed, the recovering of the lost, the healing of the sick, all this would be very feebly and faintly insinuated in "preserver." God "*preserveth* man and beast," but he is the "Savior" of his own, in a far more inward and far tenderer sense. For some time the Latin Christian writers were in considerable perplexity how they should render the Greek word, employing "salutare," "sospitator," and other terms more unsatisfactory still. The strong good sense of Augustine, however, finally disposed of the difficulty. He made no scruple about employing "salvator;" observing well, and with a true insight into the law of the growth of words, that it was not good Latin before the Savior came; but when he came, he made it to be such;

* Hoc [σωτήρ] quantum est? ita magnum ut Latinè uno verbo exprimi non possit.

for as shadows follow substances, so words result from things.*

These are, as I said, the most illustrious examples of the coming in of a new world of thoughts and feelings into the bosom of humanity, whereby has been necessitated a corresponding creation in the world of words, their outward representatives. And the same has repeated itself continually since; each new reception of the Word of life by another people must needs bring over again the same effects with more or less striking features. It is true we are not so favorably placed for tracing these effects as in the cases of the two classical languages of antiquity: yet our missionaries, to whom the study of language is in many respects so greatly indebted, have incidentally told us much on this subject, and, were their attention particularly directed to it, might doubtless tell us much more.

But it is not only when new truth directly from God has thus to fit itself to the lips of men, that such enlargements of speech follow, but in each further unfolding of those seminal truths implanted in man's heart at the first, in each new enlargement of his

* *Serm.* 299, 6: "Christus Jesus, id est Christus Salvator: hoc est enim Latinè Jesus. Nec quærant grammatici quàm sit Latinum, sed Christiani, quàm verum. Salus enim Latinum nomen est: salvare et salvator non fuerunt hæc Latina, antequam veniret Salvator: quando ad Latinos venit, et hæc Latina fecit. Cf. *De Trin.* xiii. 10: Quod verbum [salvator] Latina lingua antea non habebat, sed habere poterat; sicut potuit quando voluit."

sphere of knowledge, outward or inward, lie the same necessities involved. The beginnings and progressive advances of moral philosophy in Greece, the transplanting of the same to Rome, the rise of the scholastic, and then of the mystic theology in the middle ages, the discoveries of modern science and natural philosophy, all these have been accompanied with corresponding extensions in the limits of language. Of the words to which each of these has in turn given birth, many, it is true, have never passed beyond their own peculiar sphere, having remained technical, scientific, or purely theological to the last; but many also have passed over from the laboratory, the school, and the pulpit, into daily life, and have, with the ideas which they incorporate, become the common heritage of all. For, however hard and repulsive a front any study or science may seem to present to the great body of those who are as laymen to it, there is yet inevitably such a detrition as this going forward in the case of each, and it would not be a little interesting for one who was furnished with the knowledge sufficient, to trace it in all.

Where the movement is a great popular one, stirring the heart and mind of a people to its very depths, such as the first reception of the Christian faith, there these new words will be for the most part born out of their bosoms, a free spontaneous birth, seldom or never capable of being referred to one man more than another, because they belong to all. Where on the contrary, the movement is not so, is more strictly theological, or finds place in those regions of science and philosophy, where as first pioneers and discoverers only a few can bear their parts, there the additions and extensions will lack something of the freedom, the unconscious boldness, which marked the others. Their character will be more artificial, less spontaneous, although here also the creative genius of the single man, as there of the nation, will oftentimes set its mark; and many a single word will come forth, which shall be the result of profound meditation, or of intuitive genius, or of both in happiest combination—many a word, which shall as a torch illuminate vast regions comparatively obscure before, and, it may be, cast its rays far into the darkness beyond; or which, summing up into itself all the acquisitions in a particular direction, of the past, shall be as a mighty vantage ground from which to advance to new conquests in the realms of mind, or of nature, as yet unsubdued to the intellect of man.

As occupying something of a middle place between those more deliberate word-makers, and the people whose words rather grow than are made, we must not omit him who is a maker by the very right of his name—I mean, the poet. That creative energy with which he is endowed will in all probability manifest itself in this region as in others. Extending the domain of thought and feeling, he will scarcely fail to extend that also of language, which does not willingly lag behind. And the loftier his moods, the more of this maker he will be. The passion of such times, the all-fusing imagination, will at once suggest and justify audacities in speech, upon which in calmer moods he would not venture, or, if he ventured, would fail to carry others with him: for only the fluent metal runs easily into novel shapes and moulds. It is not merely that the old and the familiar will often become new in his hands; that will give the stamp of allowance, as to him it will be free to do, to words, should he count them worthy, which hitherto have lived only on the lips of the multitude, or been confined to some single dialect and province; but he will enrich his native tongue with words unknown and non-existent before—non-existent, that is, save in their elements; for in the historic period of a language it is not permitted to any man to bring new roots into it, but only to work on already given materials; to evolve what is latent therein, to combine what is apart, to recall what has fallen out of sight.

But to return to the more deliberate coining of words. This will often find place for the supplying of discovered deficiencies in a language. The manner in which men most often become aware of such deficiencies, is through the comparison of their own language with another and a richer, a comparison which is forced upon them, so that they can not put it by, when it becomes necessary for them to express in their own tongue that which has already found utterance in another, and so has, at any rate, shown that it is utterable in human speech. Without such a comparison, the existence of the want would probably have seldom dawned even on the most thoughtful. For language is to so great an extent the condition and limit of thought, men are so little accustomed, indeed so little able, to meditate on things, except through the intervention and by the machinery of words, that nothing short of this would bring them to a sense of the actual existence of any such wants. And it is, I may observe, one of the advantages of acquaintance with another language besides our own, and of the institution which will follow, if we have learned that other to any purpose, of these comparisons, that we thus come to be aware that names are not, and least of all the names which any single language possesses, co-extensive with things (and by "things" I mean subjects as well as objects of thought whatever one can *think* about), that a multitude of things exist which, though capable of being resumed in a word, are yet without one, unnamed and unregistered; so that, vast as is the world of names, the world of realities is even vaster still. Such discoveries the Romans made, when they attempted to transplant the moral philosophy of Greece to an Italian soil; they found that many of its words had no equivalents in their own tongue, which equivalents therefore they proceeded with more or less success to devise for themselves, appealing, with this view, to the latent capacities of their own tongue. For example, the Greek schools had a word, and one playing no unimportant part in some of their systems, to express the absence of all passion and pain. As it was absolutely necessary to possess a corresponding word, Cicero invented "idolentia," as the "if I may so speak" with which he paves the way to his first introduction of it, manifestly declares.*

Sometimes, indeed, such a skilful mintmaster of words, such a subtle watcher and weigher of their forces† as he was, will note, even without this comparison with other languages, an omission in his own, which thereupon he will endeavor to supply. Thus was it with him in regard of "invidentia." While there existed in the Latin two adjectives which, though sometimes confusedly used, had yet each its peculiar meaning, "invidus," one who is envious, "invidiosus," one who excites envy in others, there was only one substantive, "invidia," correlative to them both; with the disadvantage therefore of being employed now in an active, now in a passive sense, now for the envy which men feel, and now for that which they excite. The word he saw was made to do double duty, and that under a seeming unity there lurked a real dualism, from which manifold confu-

* *Fin.* 2, 4.

† Ille verborum vigilantissimus appensor ac mensor, as Augustine happily terms him.

sions might follow. He therefore devised "invidentia," to express the active envy, or the envying, no doubt desiring that "invidia" should be restrained to the passive, the being envied. To all appearance the word came to supply a real want, yet he did not succeed in giving it currency — indeed does not seem himself to have much cared to employ it again.*

We see by this example that it is not every word which even a great master of language proposes, that finds acceptance.† He must be contented, if some live, that others should fall to the ground. Nor is this the only one which Cicero unsuccessfully proposed. His "indolentia," which I mentioned just now, hardly passed beyond himself: his "vitiositas"‡ not at all. "Beatitas," too, and "beatitudo,"§ both of his coining, but which he owns to have something strange and uncouth about them, can hardly be said to have found more than the faintest echo in the classical literature of Rome: "beatitudo," indeed, obtained a home, as it deserved to do, in the Christian church, but the other made no way whatsoever. I do not suppose that Coleridge's "esemplastic" will find any considerable favor; while the words of Jeremy Taylor, of such Latinists as Sir Thomas

* *Tusc.* 3, 9; 4, 8. Cf. Döderlein's *Synon.* v. 3, p. 68.

† Quintilian's advice to those who come after is excellent here (1, 6, 42: "Etiamsi potest nihil peccare, qui utitur iis verbis quæ summi auctores tradiderunt, multùm tamen refert non solùm quid *dixerint*, sed etiam quid *persuaserint*."

‡ *Tusc.* 4. 15.

§ *Nat. Deor.* 1. 34.

Browne, and of others, that were born only to die, are multitudinous as the leaves of autumn. Still even the word which fails is often, though not always, an honorable testimony to the scholarship, the range of thought, the imagination of its proposer; and Ben Jonson is overhard on "neologists," if I may bring this term back to its earlier meaning, when he says: "A man coins not a new word without some peril, and less fruit; for if it happen to be received, the praise is but moderate; if refused, the scorn is assured."

But I alluded just now to comprehensive words, which should singly be effectual to say that which hitherto it had taken many words to say, in which a higher term has been reached than before had been found. It is difficult to estimate too highly the value of such words for the facilitating of mental processes, and indeed for the making practicable of many, which would have been nearly or quite impracticable without them; and those who have invented, or who have succeeded in putting into circulation such, may be esteemed as benefactors of a high order to knowledge. In the ordinary traffic of life, unless our dealings were on the smallest scale, we should willingly have about us our money in the shape rather of silver than of copper; and if our transactions were at all extensive, rather in gold than in silver; while if we were setting forth upon a long and arduous journey, we should be best pleased to turn even our gold coin itself into bills of exchange or circular notes; in fact, into the highest denomination of money which it was capable of assuming. How many words with which we are now perfectly familiar are for us what bills of exchange or circular notes are for the merchant and the traveller. As in one of these last, innumerable pence, a multitude of shillings, not a few pounds, are gathered up and represented, so have we in some single words the quintessence and final result of an infinite number of anterior mental processes, ascending one above the other, and all of which have been at length summed up for us in them. We may compare such words to some great river, which does not bring its flood of waters to the sea, till many rills have been swallowed up in brooks, and brooks in streams, and streams in tributary rivers, each of these having lost its individual being in that which at last does at once represent and is continent of them all.

Let us only consider all which must have gone before, ere the word "circle," with its corresponding idea, could have come into existence; and then consider if, each time that in some long and difficult mathematical problem we had to refer to the figure so named, we were obliged to introduce the entire definition of it, because no single word stood for it —and not this only, but the definition of each term employed in the definition—how impossible or nearly impossible it would be to carry the whole process in the mind, or to take oversight of its steps. Imagine a few more words struck out of the vocabulary of the mathematician, and if all mental activity in his direction was not quite put a stop to, yet would it be as effectually restricted as commerce and exchange would be, if all transactions had to be carried on with iron or copper as the only medium of mercantile intercourse.

It is not to be supposed that words of such primary, almost vital necessity for the science whereto they pertain as that I have just referred to, still wait to be coined; but yet, wherever knowledge is progressive, words are keeping pace with it, which with more or less felicity resume in themselves very much of the labors of the past, at once assist and abridge the labors of the future; being as tools which, themselves the result of the finest mechanical skill, do at the same time render other and further triumphs of art possible, which would have been quite unattainable without them.

But it is not merely the widening of men's intellectual horizon, which, as it brings new thoughts within the range of their vision, constrains the origination of corresponding words; but when regions of this outward world hitherto closed are laid open to them, the various novel objects of interest which these contain will demand to find their names, and not merely to be catalogued in the nomenclature of science, but in so far as they present themselves to the popular eye, will require a popular name. As however nothing is rarer in this world than the invention of aught which is entirely new, men will most often content themselves with applying to this new a name drawn from that old wherewith they are already familiar, which resembles it the most. Yet this may be done with modifications and combinations, which shall vindicate for it an original character. Thus when the Romans became acquainted with the stately giraffe, long concealed from them in the inner wilds of Africa, and we learn from Pliny that they first made this acquaintance in the shows exhibited by Julius Cæsar, it was happily imagined to designate a creature combining, though with infinitely more grace, yet something of the height and even the proportions of the camel with the spotted skin of the leopard, by a name which should incorporate both these its most prominent features,* calling it the "camelopard;" nor can we, I think, hesitate to accept his account as the true one, who describes the word as no artificial creation of the scientific naturalist, but as bursting extempore from the lips of the populace at the first moment when the novel creature was presented to their gaze. "Cerf-volant," a name which the French so happily gave to the horned scarabeus, the same which we somewhat less poetically call the "stagbeetle," is

* Varro: "Quod erat figurâ ut camelus, maculis ut panthera."

another example of what may be effected with the old materials, by merely bringing them into new combinations.

Let us take another example, and one which will present us with another proof of that which we have been called already to notice, namely, the popular birth of a multitude of words, and those the most genuine which rise up in a language; an example also of the manner in which at some periods of its growth everything turns to good, so that mistakes and errors, misshaping, and it would seem marring a word at its formation, yet do not hinder it from forming a worthy portion of the after-tongue. When the alligator, this ugly crocodile of the new world, was first seen by the Spanish discoverers, they called it, with a true insight into its species, "el lagarto," or "*the* lizard," as being the largest of that species to which it belonged. In Sir Walter Raleigh's *Discovery of Guiana*, the word still retains this its Spanish form. Sailing up the Orinoco, "We saw in it," he says, "divers sorts of strange fishes of marvellous bigness, but for *lagartos* it exceeded; for there were thousands of these ugly serpents, and the people call it, for the abundance of them, the river of *lagartos*, in their [the Spanish] language." We can perfectly explain the shape which afterward the word assumed, by supposing that English sailors who brought home the word, and had continually heard, but may probably have never seen it written, blended, as has not unfrequently happened, the Spanish article "el" with the name, and thus from this absorption of the article it acquired the shape in which we possess it now. In Ben Jonson, who writes "aligarta," we see the word in the process of its transformation.*

One of the most legitimate methods by which a language may increase in wealth, especially in the times, when its generative energy is in great part spent, as after a certain period is the case with all, is through the reviving of old words, not, that is, without discrimination, but of such as are worthy to be revived; which yet through carelessness, or ill-placed fastidiousness, or a growing unacquaintance on the part of a later generation with the elder worthies of the language, or some other cause, have been suffered to drop. These words, obsolete or obsolescent, it will sometimes happen that some writer instructed in the early literature of his native language is not willing to let die, and himself using or suggesting to the use of others, is successful in again

* I can not remember any other examples of this curious absorption of the article in English, though probably there are such; but two in French present themselves to me. "Lierre," which is "ivy," was written in early French, as by Ronsard, "l'hierre," which is no doubt correct, being from the Latin "hedera;" but "loutre," the otter, which Ampère supposes to have been originally "l'outre," is manifestly the Latin, "lutra." "La Pouille," a name given to the southern extremity of Italy, and in which we recognise "Apulia," is another variety of error, but moving in the same sphere.

putting into circulation.* And to the poet more than any other it will be thus free to recall and recover the forgotten treasures of his native language. Yet if success is to attend his attempt, or that of any other, the words to which it is thus sought to impart a second life must scarcely belong to the hoar antiquities of the language, with the dust of many centuries upon them, being not merely out of use, but out of all memory as well. A word which has not been employed since Chaucer is in a very different position from one that has only dropped out of active service since Spenser or Shakspere, and which, being found in their writings, or in those of their great compeers, has preserved for the circle of educated readers a certain vitality. Thus, if I might dissent from a great living master of English, I should doubt the employment of such "Chaucerisms," to use Ben Jonson's phrase on this very subject, as "to burgeon," as I should quite despair even of his effecting that, which of course he must look forward to in using it, namely, the giving to it cur-

* A modern French writer of some eminence, Charles Nodier, has composed a treatise on the subject of words in his own language which have become obsolete, and ought to be revived. We have a curious proof of the unobserved manner in which this sometimes is accomplished in the fact that "vaillant," which certainly now is not felt to have anything archaic about it, was seriously found fault with, as out of date, when employed in the epitaph of Turenne. Horace, too, a great observer of the fortunes of words, who has said more and wiser things about them in a few lines of his *De Arte Poeticâ* than ever have been said elsewhere, gives this as his conviction: "Multa renascentur, quæ jam cecidere."

rency again. But the case is altogether different with words which have been only recently lost, or in some sense not lost at all—such words, for example, as "leer," "lese," "debonair," "deft," "malapert," "phantast," which I instance, as every one of them to my mind worthy to have continued. The case is different, because of these some have never gone out of use among our humbler classes, so often the conservators of precious words and genuine idioms: thus you all probably know very well that "leer" is with our rustic population in the south a commoner word than "empty;" "to lese," very much more in use than "to glean;" indeed this last is scarcely known. Others again, as "deft," "debonair," "malapert," reach down, at least in literary use, to the middle of the eighteenth century, with, in the case of the last, the further inconvenience entailed by its loss, that we have been obliged to make "pert" which remains do double duty, that of "malapert" and its own. For as some word is plainly wanting, not so strong as "insolent," we have been led to employ "pert" exclusively in an unfavorable sense, while yet it was free of old to use it also in a good, even as among our southern poor it still retains the meaning of "sprightly" or "lively;" a child recovering from illness, a cagebird after moulting, are said to look quite "pert" again—an employment of the word justified by Shakspere's

"Awake the *pert* and nimble spirit of youth."

Other and less honorable causes than many of those which I have sought hitherto to trace, give birth to new words; and it will happen that the character and moral condition of an epoch are only too plainly revealed by the new words which have risen up in that period, upon which sometimes they reflect back a very fearful light. Thus a great Latin historian tells us of the Roman emperor, Tiberius, one of those "inventors of evil things" to whom St. Paul alludes (Rom. i. 30), that he caused words unknown before to emerge in the Latin tongue, for the setting out of wickedness, happily also previously unknown, which he had invented.

The atrocious attempt of Louis the Fourteenth to convert to Romanism the protestants in his dominions by quartering dragoons upon them, with all license to misuse to the uttermost those who would not apostatize from their faith, this "booted mission" (mission bottée), as it was facetiously called, has bequeathed "dragonade" to the French language. I believe "refugee" had about the same time its rise, being first applied to those who escaped the tender mercies of these missionaries.

And "roué," a word to a considerable extent naturalized among us, throws light upon a curious though a shameful page of history. It is a term applied, as we may be aware, to a man of profligate character and conduct; but properly and primarily means one "wheeled," or broken on the wheel.

Now the first person who gave it its secondary meaning, was the profligate duke of Orleans, regent of France in the interval between the reigns of Louis the Fourteenth and Fifteenth. It was his miserable pride to collect around him companions as worthless and wicked as himself, and he called them his "roués," inasmuch as there was not one of them that did not deserve, as he was wont to boast, to be broken on the wheel, that being then in France the punishment for the worst malefactors.* When we have learned the pedigree of the word, the man and the age which gave it birth rise up before us, glorying in their shame, and no longer caring to pay even that outward hypocritical homage, which vice yields often to virtue.

The great French Revolution has made also its contributions to the French language; and these contributions characteristic enough. We know much of that event, when we know that among other words it gave birth to these, "incivisme," "sansculotte," "noyade," "guillotine." And still later, the French conquests in North Africa, and the pitiless methods by which every attempt at resistance on the part of the free tribes of the interior has been put down and punished, all this has left its mark upon the language; for it has added to it the

* The "roués" themselves declared that the word expressed rather their readiness to give any proof of their affection, even to the being broke upon the wheel, to their protector and friend.

word "razzia," to express the sweeping and sudden destruction of a tribe, its herds, its crops, and all that belongs to it—a word bearing on its front that it is not originally of French formation, having rather an Italian physiognomy, but being, I believe, the popular corruption of an Arabic word—one of which the language therefore may be as little proud, as the people of the thing which is indicated by it.

But it would ill become us to look only abroad for examples of that whereof perhaps at least an equal abundance may be found much nearer home, and it must at once be acknowledged that there are words also among ourselves, which preserve a record of passages in our history in which we have little reason to glory. "Plunder" was a word first heard of in England in the period immediately preceding our civil wars, between 1630 and 1640. Richardson, whose *Dictionary* has in most cases the passage in English literature which best serves to mark the exact epoch of a word's appearing, as well as the circumstances which attended its rise, has passed over two instructive passages in Fuller in regard of this. He observes with truth that the word began to be in common use at the commencement of the Great Rebellion. The word is German, for this Fuller means, when he calls it "Dutch," and he ascribes the first bringing of it in to the soldiers who returned from the campaigns of Gustavus Adolphus. "Sure I am," he says, "we first heard thereof in the Swedish wars;

and if the name and thing be sent back whence it came, few English eyes would weep thereat."* The "thing" was not exactly what it is now; it was not the spoiling by an open violence, but the ransacking and robbing which under legal pretence as of searching for papers found place, of the effects of the so-called "malignants;" so that "plunderings and sequestrations" are named continually together. "Delinquent" belongs to the same epoch.

"Mob," too, and "sham," had their birth in one of the most shameful periods of English history, that between the Restoration and Revolution. The first of these words originated in a certain club in London in the latter end of the reign of Charles the Second. "I may note," says a writer of the time, "that the rabble first changed their title, and were called the 'mob' in the assemblies of this [the Green Ribbon] club. It was their beast of burden, and called first 'mobile vulgus,' but fell naturally into the contraction of one syllable, and ever since is become proper English."† Yet we find considerably later a writer in *The Spectator* speaking of "mob" as still only struggling into existence. "I dare not answer," he says, "that mob, rap, pos, incog., and the like will not in time be looked at as part of our tongue." In regard of "mob," abbrevi-

* *Church History*, b. 11, § 4, 33; cf. b. 9, § 4, quite at the beginning.

† North's *Examen*, p. 574. If we may trust the origin of "sham" which he gives, p. 231, it is not less disgraceful than the word itself

ated as we see from "mobile," the multitude swayed hither and thither by each gust of passion or caprice, this, which that writer plainly hardly expected, while he confessed it possible, has actually taken place. "It is one of the many words formerly slang, which are now used by our best writers, and received, like pardoned outlaws, into the body of respectable citizens."

And though the murdering of poor helpless lodgers, afterward to sell their bodies to the surgeons for dissection, can not be regarded as a crime in which the nation had a share, or anything but the monstrous wickedness of one or two, yet the word "to burk," drawn from the name of a wretch who long pursued this hideous traffic, a word which has won its place in the language, will be a lasting memorial in all after-times, unless indeed its origin should be forgotten, to how strange a crime this age of a boasted civilization could give birth.

Such are some of the sources of the increase in the wealth of a language, or, it may be, in that which has no just title to be termed by this name. There have been, from time to time, those who have so little understood what a language and the laws of a language are — that it has a life, just as really as a man or as a tree — that, as a man, it must grow to its full stature, being also submitted to his conditions of decay — as a forest-tree, will defy any feeble bands which should attempt to control its expansion, so long as the principle of growth is in it—as a tree too will continually, while it casts off some leaves, be putting forth others—that they have sought by a decree of theirs to arrest its growth, to pronounce it to have attained to the limits of its growth and development, so that no one should henceforward presume to make additions to it. The attempt has utterly failed, even when made under the most favorable conditions for success. For instance, the French academy, containing the great body of the distinguished literary men of France, once sought to exercise such a domination over their own language, and, if any could have succeeded, might have hoped to do so. But the language recked of their decrees, as little as the advancing ocean did of those of Canute. They were obliged to give way, and in each successive edition of their dictionary to throw open its doors to words which had established themselves in the language, and would hold their ground, comparatively indifferent whether they received their seal of allowance or no.

Certainly those who make attempts of this kind strangely forget that *all* the words in a language, with the exception of its primitive roots, were at one time or another novelties. We have so taken for granted that those with which we have been always familiar, whose right to form a part of it no one dreams of challenging or disputing, being perfectly naturalized now, have always formed part of it, that we should, I believe, be somewhat startled to discover of how very late introduction not a few of them actually are, what an amount of remonstrance, and even resistance, some of them encountered at the first. To take two or three Latin examples. Cicero, in employing "favor," a word in a little while after used by everybody, does it with an apology, seems to feel that he is introducing a questionable novelty; "urbanus," too, in our sense of "urbane," had only just come up; "obsequium" he believes Terence to have been the first to employ.* "Soliloquium" seems to us so natural, indeed so necessary, a word, this "soliloquy," or talking of a man with himself, something which would so inevitably seek out its suitable expression, that it is hard to persuade oneself that no one spoke of a soliloquy before Augustine, that the word should have been invented, as he distinctly informs us, by himself.†

And to take some English examples: Sir Thomas Elyot (1534) speaks of the now familiar words "frugality," "temperance," "sobriety," "magnanimity," as being not in his day in general use; "magnanimity," however, is in Chaucer. The translators of the authorized version of the Bible, in a preface not now often reprinted, but prefixed to the original edition, find fault, and others had done the same before them, with the Greek and Latin words—"inkhorn terms,"

* On the new words in classical Latin see Quintilian viii. 3, 30–37

† *Solil.* 2, 7.

Fulke calls them—with which the Rhemish translators so plentifully sprinkled their version; with the intention, as these last affirmed, of preserving for it an ecclesiastical character; but as others, and we can scarcely say uncharitably, charged them, that so, if they must give the Scriptures in the vulgar tongue, they might yet keep them, as far as might be, "dark and unprofitable to the ignorant readers." In many cases the accusation was quite borne out by the facts, and the Greek and Latin terms they employed could never have made themselves at home in English; but this certainly is not so in all. Thus "rational," "tunic," "scandal," "neophyte," were severally either words which had not been invented by the Rhemish translators, having existed long before; or the sequel has gone far to justify them in what they did, the words having been freely absorbed into the language, as useful additions to it. "To evangelize" was another word which they were blamed for introducing. It was quite worthy to have been introduced, supposing it had not previously been in being; but it already found place in Wiclif's version, as at Luke i. 19, xvi. 16, which the Rhemish merely follows, so that Fulke is every way unjust in urging against the authors of this: "When you say '*evangelized*,' you do not translate, but feign a new word, which is not understood of mere English ears."

Considering how old a *thing* is selfishness in the world, we should hardly have expected to find "selfish" to be a word of such late devising as it proves. From a passage in Hacket's *Life of Archbishop Williams*, we certainly conclude that it had only newly come up in his time, and been freshly issued from the puritan mint.* "Mob" is of still later date, belonging, as we saw just now, to the latter half of the seventeenth century. "Coffee" and "tea" were not naturalized words in Locke's time, at least not in 1684. He writes "Coffé," "thé."† "Tour" is printed "toùr" so late as 1712. "Pretentious," the adjective of "pretence," which is a word at the present moment forcing its way into existence, is now displeasing enough to delicate ears, yet no doubt it will keep its ground, for it supplies a real need, and has the analogy of the French "pretentieux" to help it; in a very little while multitudes will use it, quite unconscious that it is not older, nor perhaps so old as they are themselves.

When a word has proved an unquestionable gain to the language, it is very interesting to preside, so to speak, at its birth, to watch it as it first comes forth, timid, and it may be as yet doubtful of the reception it will meet with; and the interest is very much enhanced, if it thus come forth on some memorable occasion, or from some memorable man. Both

* Hacket's *Life of Archbishop Williams*, part 2, p. 144: "When they [the presbyterians] saw that he was not *selfish* (it is a word of their own new mint)," &c.

† Locke's *Diary*, in his *Life* by Lord King, p. 42.

these interests meet in the word "essay." If any one were asked what is the most remarkable volume of essays which the world has seen, few, having sufficient oversight of the field of literature to be capable of replying, would fail to answer, Lord Bacon's. But they were also the first which bore that name; for we certainly gather from the following passage in the (intended) dedication of the volume to Prince Henry, that the word "essay" was altogether a very recent one in the English language, and in the use to which he put it, perfectly novel: he says: "To write just treatises requireth leisure in the writer, and leisure in the reader; . . . which is the cause which hath made me choose to write certain brief notes set down rather significantly than curiously, which I have called *Essays*. The word is late, but the thing is ancient." From these words, and others which I have omitted in the quotation, we further gather that little as "essays" at the present day can be considered a word of modesty, deprecating too large expectations on the part of the reader, it had, as "sketches" perhaps would have now, such an ethical significance in this its earliest use. In this last respect it resembled the "philosopher" of Pythagoras. Before his time the founders of systems of philosophy had styled themselves, or been willing to be styled by others, "wise men." This appellation, "lover of wisdom," so modest and so beautiful, was of his devising.

Let us remark, at the same time, that while thus

some words surprise us that they are so new, others again that they are so old. Few, I should imagine, are aware that the word "rationalist," and this in a theological, and not merely a philosophical sense, is of such early date as it is; or that we have not imported quite in these later times both the name and the thing from Germany. This, however, is very far from being in either respect the case. There was a sect of "rationalists" in the time of the Commonwealth, who called themselves such exactly on the same grounds as those who in later times have challenged the name. Thus, one writing the news from London,* among other things, mentions:—

"There is a new sect sprung up among them [the presbyterians and independents], and these are the *rationalists*, and what their reason dictates them in church or state stands for good, until they be convinced with better;" with more to the same effect. The word "Christology" a recent reviewer has characterized as a monstrous importation from Germany. I should be quite ready to agree with him that English theology does not need, and can do excellently well without it; yet is it not this absolute novelty: for in the *preface* to the works of that great divine of the seventeenth century, Thomas Jackson, written by a friend and scholar, the following passage occurs: "The reader will find in this author an emi-

* With date, Oct. 14, 1646; in *The Clarendon State Papers*, v. 2, p. 40, of the *Appendix*.

nent excellence in that part of divinity which I make bold to call *Christology*, in displaying the great mystery of godliness, God the Son manifested in human flesh."*

In their power of taking up foreign or otherwise new words into healthy circulation and making them truly their own, languages are very different as compared with one another, and the same language is very different from itself at different periods of its life. There are languages of which the appetite and digestive power, the assimilative energy, is at some periods almost unlimited. Nothing is too hard for them; they will shape and mould to their own uses and habits almost whatsoever is offered to them. This is in the youth of a language; as age advances upon it, this assimilative power diminishes. Words are still adopted; for this process of adoption can never cease, but a chemical amalgamation of the new with the old does not any longer find place, or only in some instances, and partially in them. They lie often on the surface of the language; their sharp corners are not worn and rounded off; they remain foreign still in their aspect and outline, and, having missed the great opportunity of becoming otherwise, will remain so to the end. Those who adopt, as with an inward misgiving about their own gift and power of stamping them afresh, seem to make a conscience of keeping them in exactly the same form in which

* *Preface to Dr. Jackson's Works*, v. 1, p. xxvii.

they have received them; instead of conforming them to the laws of that new community into which they now have been received. Nothing will illustrate this better, or indeed so well as a comparison of different words of the same family, which have at different periods been introduced into our language. We shall find that those of an earlier introduction have become English through and through, while the later introduced belonging to the same group, have been very far from undergoing the same transforming process. Thus "bishop," a word as old as the introduction of Christianity into England, though not hiding its descent from "episcopus," is thoroughly English; while "episcopal," which has supplanted "bishoply," is only a Latin word in an English dress. "Alms," too, is genuine English, and English which has descended to us from far; the very shape in which we have the word, one syllable for "eleemosyna" of six, sufficiently testifying this; "letters," as Horne Tooke observes, "like soldiers, being apt to desert and drop off in a long march." I need not say that the long and awkward "eleemosynary" is of a very much more recent date. Or sometimes this comparison is still more striking, when it is not merely words of the same family, but the very same word which has been twice adopted, at an earlier period and a later—the earlier form will be truly English, as "palsy;" the later will be only a Greek or Latin word spelt with English letters, as "paralysis." "Dropsy," "megrim," "tansy," and many more words that one might name, have nothing of strangers or foreigners about them, have made themselves quite at home in English; so entirely is their physiognomy native that it would be difficult even to suspect that they were of Greek descent as they are. Nor has "kickshaws" anything about it now which would compel us at once to recognise in it the French "quelques choses" "French *kickshose*," as with allusion to the quarter from which it came, and while the memory of that was yet fresh in men's minds, it was often called by our early writers.

An eminent German grammarian has called attention to a very curious process which he traces many German words to have undergone in the act of their adoption from foreign tongues, whereby not only their outward form and shape are fitted and moulded to their new home, but a new soul, a new principle of life put within them. What he means will best be understood by a single illustration. The Germans, knowing nothing of carbuncles, had naturally no word of their own for them, and when they first became acquainted with them, as naturally borrowed the Latin term "carbunculus," which originally had meant "a little live coal," to designate these precious stones of a fiery red. But "carbunculus," though a real word, full of poetry and life, for a Latin, would have been only an arbitrary sign for others, ignorant of that language. What then did they do? or what, rather did the working genius of the language do? It adopted, but in adopting modified slightly the word, changing it into "kar funkel," thus retaining the outlines of the original, yet at the same time, inasmuch as "funkeln" signifies "to sparkle," reproducing now in an entirely novel manner the image of the bright sparkling of the stone, for every knower of his native tongue.

I have no doubt that our own language would supply instances of a like kind, though I have not any such at the present to adduce to you; which not having, I must be content with one which the French seems to supply me. "Rossignol," a nightingale, is undoubtedly derived from the Latin "lusciniola," the diminutive of "luscinia," with the alteration which so frequently finds place in the romance languages, of the commencing *l* into *r*. Whatever may be the etymology of "luscinia," whether it be "in lucis cano," the singer in the groves, or "lugens cano," the melancholy singer, or, as is most probable, "luscus cano," the singer in the twilight, with which our "nightingale" would most closely correspond, it is plain that for Frenchmen the word would no longer be suggestive of any of these meanings, hardly even for French scholars, after the serious transformations which it had undergone; while yet, at the same time, in the exquisitely musical "rossignol," and still more, perhaps, in the Italian "usignuolo," there is an evident intention and endeavor to express something of the music of the bird's song in the liquid melody of the imitative name which it bears; and thus to put a new soul into the word, in lieu of that one which it has lost.

One of the most striking facts about new words, and a very signal testimony of their birth from the bosom of the people, that is, where they are not plainly from the schools, is the difficulty which is so often found in tracing their derivation. When the *causæ vocum* are sought, which they justly are, and out of much more than mere curiosity, for the *causæ rerum* are very often contained in them, they continually elude research; and this, not merely where attention has only been called to the words, and interest about their etymology excited, long after they had been in popular use, and when thus they had left their origin, whatever it may have been, very far behind them—for that the words of a remote antiquity should often puzzle and perplex us, should give scope to idle guesses, or altogether defy conjecture, this is nothing strange—but even when it has been sought to investigate their origin almost as soon as they have come into existence. Their rise is mysterious; like so many other acts of *becoming*, it is veiled in deepest obscurity. They appear, they are in everybody's mouth; but yet when it is inquired whence they are, nobody can tell. They are but of yesterday, and yet with a marvellous rapidity have forgotten the circumstances of their origin. Thus Baxter tells us in his most instructive *Narrative of his Life and Times*, that there already existed two theories about the term "roundheads,"* a word not nearly so old as himself, showing how much uncertainty already rested upon it. "Cannibal," as a designation of man-eating savages, came first into use with the great discoveries in the western world of the fifteenth and sixteenth centuries. I know not whether it occurs earlier than in Hackluyt's *Voyages*. All attempts to explain it have been fruitless. So, too, the origin of "huguenots," as applied to the French protestants, was already a matter of doubt and discussion in the lifetime of those who first bore it.† One might suppose that a name like "Canada," given, and within fresh historic times, to a vast territory, would be accounted for, but it is not; or that the Anglo-Americans would be able to explain how they got their word "caucus," which plays so prominent a part in their elections, but they can not.

* "The original of which name is not certainly known. Some say it was because the puritans then commonly wore short hair, and the king's party long hair; some say, it was because the queen, at Strafford's trial, asked who that roundheaded man was, meaning Mr. Pym, because he spake so strongly."—P. 34.

† I can hardly doubt that it is a corruption of "eidgnoten," low German for "eidgenossen," confederates; but this was not the explanation of some who must have been grown men at the time of its first emerging.

These are but a handful of examples of the way in which words forget the circumstances of their birth. Now if we could believe in any merely *arbitrary* words, such, that is, as stood in connection with nothing but the mere lawless caprice of some inventor, the impossibility of tracing their derivations would be nothing strange. Indeed it would be lost labor to seek for the parentage of all words, when many perhaps had not any. But there is no such thing; there is no word which is not, as the Spanish gentleman loves to call himself, an "hidalgo," the son of somebody; all are the embodiment, more or less successful, of a sensation, a thought, or a fact; or if of more fortuitous birth, still they attach themselves somewhere to the already subsisting world of words and things, and have their point of contact with it and departure from it, not always discoverable, as we see, but yet always existing; so that, when a word entirely refuses to give up the secret of its origin, it can be regarded in no other light but as a riddle which no one has succeeded in solving, a lock of which no one has found the key — but still a riddle which has a solution, a lock for which there is a key, though now, it may be, irrecoverably lost. And this fact of the difficulty, often the impossibility of tracing the genealogy even of words of a very recent formation, is, as I said, an evidence of the birth at least of these out of the heart and from the lips of the people. Had they had their rise first in books, then it would be easily traced; had it been from the schools of the learned, these would not have failed to have left a recognisable stamp and mark upon them.

But we must conclude. I may have seemed in this present lecture a little to have outrun your needs, and to have sometimes moved in a sphere too remote from that in which your future work will lie. Perhaps it may have been so; yet is it in truth very difficult to say of any words that they do not touch us, that they do not reach us in their influence, or in some way bear upon our studies, upon that which we shall hereafter have to teach or shall desire to learn; that there are any conquests which language makes, that concern only a few, and may be regarded indifferently by all others. For it is here as with many inventions in the arts and luxuries of life, which being in the beginning the exclusive privilege and possession of the wealthy, the cultivated, the refined, do yet gradually descend into lower strata of society, until at length what were once the luxuries and elegancies of a few, have become the decencies, well nigh the necessities of all. Exactly in the same manner there are words, once only on the lips of philosophers or divines, of the deeper thinkers of their time, or of those interested in their speculations, which yet step by step have come down, not debasing themselves in this act of becoming popular, but training and elevating more and more to understand

and embrace their meaning, till at length they have become truly a part of the nation's common stock, household words used naturally and easily by all.

And I know not how I can better conclude this lecture than by quoting some words which express with a rare eloquence all which I have been laboring to utter: for this truth, which many indeed have noticed, none that I am aware of have set forth with at all the same fullness of illustration, or laying upon it at all the same stress, as the author of *The Philosophy of the Inductive Sciences*, whose words now quoted are but one out of many passages on the same theme: "Language is often called an instrument of thought, but it is also the nutriment of thought; or, rather, it is the atmosphere in which thought lives; a medium essential to the activity of our speculative powers, although invisible and imperceptible in its operation; and an element modifying, by its qualities and changes, the growth and complexion of the faculties which it feeds. In this way the influence of preceding discoveries upon subsequent ones, of the past upon the present, is most penetrating and universal, although most subtle and difficult to trace. The most familiar words and phrases are connected by imperceptible ties with the reasonings and discoveries of former men and distant times. Their knowledge is an inseparable part of ours; the present generation inherits and uses the scientific wealth of all the past. And this is the fortune, not only of the great and rich in the intellectual world, of those who have the key to the ancient storehouses, and who have accumulated treasures of their own, but the humblest inquirer, while he puts his reasonings into words, benefits by the labors of the greatest. When he counts his little wealth he finds he has in his hands coins which bear the image and superscription of ancient and modern intellectual dynasties, and that in virtue of this possession acquisitions are in his power, solid knowledge within his reach, which none could ever have attained to, if it were not that the gold of truth once dug out of the mine circulates more and more widely among mankind."

LECTURE V.

THE DISTINCTION OF WORDS.

It is to the subject of synonyms and their distinction, with the advantages which may be derived from the study of these that I propose to devote the present lecture. But what, it may be asked, do we mean, when, comparing certain words with one another, we affirm of them that they are synonyms? It is meant that they are words which, with great and essential resemblances of meaning, have at the same time small, subordinate, and partial differences—these differences being such as either originally, and on the ground of their etymology, inhered in them; or differences which they have by usage acquired in the eyes of all; or such as, though nearly latent now, they are capable of receiving at the hands of wise and discreet masters of the tongue. Synonyms are words of like significance in the main, but with a certain unlikeness as well.

So soon as the term is defined thus, it will be at once perceived by any acquainted with the derivation, that strictly speaking, it is a misnomer, and is given to these words with a certain inaccuracy and impropriety; since in strictness the terms "synonyms," or "synonymous," applied to words, would affirm of them that they covered not merely almost the same extent of meaning, but altogether and exactly the same, that they were in their signification perfectly identical and coincident. The terms, however, are not ordinarily so used, and plainly are not so, when it is undertaken to trace out the distinction between synonyms; for, without denying that there are such absolutely coincident words, such perfect synonyms, yet these could not be the object of any such discrimination; since, where there was no real distinction, it would be lost labor and the exercise of a perverse ingenuity to attempt to draw one. Synonyms, then as the word is generally understood, and as I shall use it here, are words with slighter differences already existing between them, or with the capabilities of such: neither on the one side absolutely identical; but neither we may add, on the other only very remotely related to one another; for the differences between these last will be self-evident, will so lie on the surface and proclaim themselves to all, that it would be impossible to make them clearer than they already are, and it would be like holding a candle to the sun to attempt it. They must be words which are more or less liable to confusion, but which yet ought not to be confounded; words, as one has said, "quæ conjungi, non confundi, debent;" words in which there originally inhered a difference, or between which, though once absolutely identical, such has gradually grown up, and so established itself in the use of the best writers, and in the instinct of the best speakers of the tongue, that it claims to be recognised and openly admitted by all.

But here an interesting question presents itself to us, which is this: How do languages come to possess synonyms of this latter class, which are differenced not by etymology or other deep-lying and necessary distinction, but only by usage? Now if they had been made by agreement, of course no such words could exist; for when one word had been found which was the adequate representative of a feeling or an object, no further one would have been sought. But languages are the result of processes very different from, and far less formal and regular than this. Various tribes, each with its own dialect, kindred indeed, but in many respects distinct, coalesce into one people, and cast their contributions of language into a common stock; sometimes two have the same word, but in forms sufficiently different to cause that both remain, but as different words; thus in Latin, "serpo" and "repo" are merely two slightly different appropriations of the same Greek word, and of "puteo" and "fœteo" the same may be said; thus too in German, "odem" and "athem," were originally but different formations of the same word. Or again, a conquering people have fixed themselves in the midst of a conquered; they impose their dominson, but do not succeed in imposing their language; nay, being few in number, they find themselves at last compelled to adopt the language of the conquered; or after a while that which may be called a transaction, a compromise between the two languages, finds place. Thus was it in England; our modern English being in the main such a compromise between the Anglo-Saxon and the Norman-French.

These are causes of the existence of synonyms which reach far back into the history of a nation and a language; but other causes at a later period are also at work. When a written literature springs up, authors familiar with various foreign tongues, import from one and another words which are not absolutely required, which are oftentimes rather luxuries than necessities. Sometimes having a very good word of their own, they must yet needs go and look for a finer one, as they esteem it, from abroad; as, for instance, the Latin having its own good and expressive "succinum" (from "succus"), for "amber," some must import from the Greek the ambiguous "electrum." But of these which are thus proposed as candidates for admission, some fail to receive the rights of citizenship, and after longer or shorter probation are rejected; it may be, never advance beyond their first proposer. Enough, however, receive the stamp of popular allowance to create embarrassment for a while, and until their relations with the already existing words are adjusted. As a single illustration of the various quarters from which the English has thus been augmented, and in the end enriched, I would instance the words "trick," "device," "finesse," "artifice," and "stratagem," and enumerate the various sources from which we have gotten these words. Here "trick" is Saxon, "devisa" is Italian, "finesse" is French, "artificium" is Latin, and "stratagema" Greek.

By-and-by, however, as a language becomes itself more an object of attention, at the same time that society, advancing from a simpler to a more complex state, has more things to designate and thoughts to utter, it is felt to be a waste of resources to have two or more words for the signifying of one and the same object. Men feel, and rightly, that with a boundless world lying around them and demanding to be named, and which they only make their own in the measure that they do name it, with infinite shades and varieties of thought and feeling subsisting in their own minds, and claiming to find utterance in words, it is a mere and wanton extravagance to expend two or more signs on that which could adequately be set forth by one — an extravagance in one part of their expenditure, which would be almost sure to issue in, and to be punished by, a too great scantness and straitness in another. Some thought or feeling would be certain to want its adequate sign because another has two. Hereupon that which has been well called the process of "desynonymizing" begins — that is of gradually coming to discriminate in use between words which have hitherto been accounted perfectly equivalent, and, as such, indifferently employed. It is a positive enriching of a language when this process is felt to be accomplished, when two or more words which were once promiscuously used, are felt to have had each its own peculiar domain assigned to it, which it shall not itself overstep, upon which the others shall not encroach. This may seem at first sight but as the better regulation of old territory; for all practical purposes it is the acquisition of new.

It is not to be supposed that this desynonymizing process is effected according to any pre-arranged purpose or plan. The working genius of the language accomplishes its own objects, causes these synonymous words insensibly to fall off from one another, and to acquire separate and peculiar meanings. The most that any single writer can do, save indeed in matters of science, is, as has been observed, to assist an already existing inclination, to bring to the consciousness of all that which may already have been implicitly felt by many, and thus to hasten the process of this disengagement, or, as it has been excellently expressed, "to regulate and ordinate the evident nisus and tendency of the popular usage into a severe definition;" and establish on a firm basis the distinction, so that it shall not be lost sight of, or brought into question again. This, for instance, Wordsworth did in respect of the words "imagination" and "fancy." Before he wrote, it was, I suppose, obscurely felt by most that in "imagination" there was more of the earnest, in "fancy" of the play of the spirit, that the first was a loftier faculty and gift than the second; yet for all this the words were continually, and not without loss, confounded. He first, in the preface to his *Lyrical Ballads*, rendered it henceforth impossible that any one, who had read and mastered what he had written on the two words, should remain unconscious any longer of the important difference existing between them.*

* I had read a great many years ago, in The Opium Eater's *Letters to a Young Man whose Education has been neglected*, a passage which I had still clearly in my mind while writing the above. I have now recovered this passage, which, though it only says over again what is said above, yet does this so much more forcibly and fully, that I shall not hesitate to quote it, and the more readily that these letters, in many respects so valuable, have never been reprinted, but lie buried in the old numbers of a magazine, like so many other of the "disjecta membra" of this illustrious master of English prose. "All languages," he says, "tend to clear themselves of synonyms, as intellectual culture advances; the superfluous words being taken up and appropriated by new shades and combinations of thought evolved in the progress of society. And long before this appropriation is fixed and petrified, as it were, into the acknowledged vocabulary of the language, an insensible clinamen (to borrow a Lucretian word) prepares the way for it. Thus, for instance, before Mr. Wordsworth had unveiled the great philosophic distinction between the powers of fancy and imagination, the two words had begun to diverge from each other, the first being used to express a faculty somewhat capricious and exempted from law, the other to express a faculty more self-determined. When, therefore, it was at length perceived, that under an apparent unity of meaning there lurked a real dualism, and for philosophic purposes it was necessary that this distinction should have its appropriate expression, this necessity was met half way by the *clinamen* which had already affected

Let me remark by the way how many other words in English are still waiting for such a discrimination. What an ethical gain, for instance, would it be, how much clearness would it bring into men's thoughts and feelings, if the distinction which exists in Latin between "vindicta" and "ultio," that the first is a moral act, the just punishment of the sinner by his God, of the criminal by the judge, the other an act in which the self-gratification of one who counts himself injured or offended is sought, could in like manner be established between "vengeance" and "revenge," so that only "vengeance" (with the verb "avenge") should be ascribed to God, and to men acting as the executors of his righteous doom; while all in which their evil and sinful passions are the impulsive motive should be exclusively termed "revenge." As it now is, the moral disapprobation which cleaves, and cleaves justly, to "revenge," is oftentimes transferred almost unconsciously to "vengeance;" while yet without vengeance it is impossible to conceive in an evil world any assertion of

the popular usage of the words." Compare with this what Coleridge had before said upon the subject, *Biog. Lit.*, v. 1, p. 90. It is to Coleridge we owe the word "desynonymize," and his own contributions direct and indirect in this province are perhaps both more in number, and more important, than those of any modern English writer, as for instance the disentanglement of "fanaticism" and "enthusiasm," which we mainly owe to him (*Lit. Rem.*, v. 2, p. 365), and of other words not a few; as "keenness" and "subtlety" (*Table Talk*, p. 140), "poetry" and "poesy" (*Lit. Rem.*, v. 1, p. 219); and that on which he himself laid so great a stress, "reason" and "understanding."

righteousness, any moral government whatsoever. These distinctions which still wait to be made we may fitly regard "as so much reversionary wealth in our mother-tongue."

The two causes which I mentioned above, the fact that English is in the main a compromise between the languages spoken by the Anglo-Saxon and the Norman, and the further circumstance that it has received, welcomed, and found place for many later additions, these causes have together effected that we possess in English a great many duplicates, not to speak of triplicates, or even such a quintuplicate as that which I adduced just now, where the Saxon, French, Italian, Latin, and Greek, had each given us a word. Let me mention a few duplicate substantives, Anglo-Saxon and Latin; thus we have "shepherd" and "pastor;" "feeling" and "sentiment;" "handbook" and "manual;" "shire" and "county;" "ship" and "nave;" "anger" and "ire;" "grief" and "dolor;" "feather" and "plume;" "love" and "charity;" forerunner" and "precursor;" "freedom" and "liberty;" "murder" and "homicide;" "moons" and "lunes"—a word which has not been met with in the singular. Sometimes, in science and theology especially, we have gone both to the Latin and to the Greek, and drawn the same word from them both; thus "deist" and "theist;" "numeration" and "arithmetic;" "Revelation" and "Apocalypse;" "temporal" and "chronical;" "compassion" and "sympathy;" "supposition" and "hypothesis." But to return to the Anglo-Saxon and Latin, the main factors of our tongue, beside duplicate substantives, we have duplicate verbs, such as "to heal" and "to cure;" "to whiten" and "to blanch;" "to soften" and "to mollify;" "to cloak" and "to palliate;" with many more.

Duplicate adjectives also are numerous, as "shady" and "umbrageous;" "unreadable" and "illegible;" "almighty" and "omnipotent." Occasionally where only one substantive, an Anglo-Saxon, exists, yet the adjectives are duplicate, and the English, which has not adopted the Latin substantive, has yet admitted the adjective; thus "burden" has not merely "burdensome" but also "onerous," while yet "onus" has found no place with us; "priest" has "priestly" and "sacerdotal;" "king" has "kingly," "regal," which is purely Latin, and "royal," which is Latin distilled through the Norman. "Bodily" and "corporal," "boyish" and "puerile," "bloody" and "sanguine," "fearful" and "timid," "manly" and "virile," "womanly" and "feminine," "starry" and "stellar," "yearly" and "annual," may all be placed in the same list. Nor are these more than a handful of words out of the number which might be adduced, and I think you would find both pleasure and profit in seeking to add to these lists, and as far as you are able, to make them gradually complete.

I will observe by the way, that I have only adduced instances in which both the words have continued to maintain their ground in our spoken and written language to the present day. Other cases are not few in which these duplicates once existed, but in which the one word has in the end proved fatal to, and has extinguished the other. Thus "resurrection" and "againrising" no doubt existed contemporaneously; Wiclif uses them indifferently; we may say the same of "judge" and "doomsman," "adultery" and "spouse-breach," and of many words more. In each of these cases, however, instead of dividing the intellectual domain between them, which perhaps would not always have been easy, the one word has definitively put the other out of use; the Latin word, as you will observe, has triumphed over the Anglo-Saxon. I am not of those who consider these triumphs of the Latin element of our speech to be in every case a matter of regret; though I would not willingly have seen "pavone," which Spenser would have introduced, for our much older "peacock;" or "terremote," which Gower employs, for "earthquake," or other such Latinisms as these.

But to return; if we look closely at those other words which have succeeded in maintaining side by side their ground, we shall not fail to observe that in almost every instance they have vindicated for themselves separate spheres of meaning, that although not in etymology, they have still in use become more or less distinct. Thus we use "shepherd" almost always in its primary meaning, keeper of sheep; while "pastor" is exclusively used in the tropical sense, one that feeds the flock of God; at the same time the language having only the one adjective, "pastoral," that is of necessity common to both. "Love" and "charity" are used in our authorized version of the New Testament promiscuously, and out of the sense of their equivalence are made to represent one and the same Greek word; but in modern use "charity" has come almost exclusively to signify one particular manifestation of love, the supply of the bodily needs of others, "love" continuing to express the affection of the soul. "Ship" remains in its literal meaning, while "nave" has become a symbolic term used in sacred architecture alone. So with "illegible" and "unreadable," the first is applied to the hand-writing, the second to the subject-matter written; thus, a man writes an "illegible" hand; he has published an "unreadable" book. So, too, it well becomes boys to be "boyish," but not men to be "puerile." Or take "to blanch" and "to whiten;" we have grown to use the first in the sense of to withdraw coloring matter: thus we "blanch" almonds or linen; the cheek is "blanched" with fear, that is, by the withdrawing of the blood; but we "whiten" a wall, not by the withdrawing of some other color, but by the superinducing of white;

thus "whited sepulchres." "To palliate" is not now used, though it once was, in the sense of wholly cloaking or covering over, as it might be, our sins, but in that of extenuating; "to palliate" our faults is not to hide them altogether, but to seek to diminish their guilt in part.

It might be urged that there was a certain preparedness in these words to separate off in their meaning from one another, inasmuch as they originally belonged to different stocks; nor would I say that it was not so, nor deny that this may have assisted; but we find the same process at work where difference of stock can have supplied no such assistance. "Astronomy" and "astrology" are both drawn from the Greek, nor is there any reason beforehand why the second should not be in as honorable use as the first; for it signifies the *reason*, as astronomy the *law*, of the stars. But seeing there is a true and a false science of the stars, both needing words to utter them, it has come to pass that in our later use, "astrology" designates always that pretended science of imposture, which affecting to submit the moral freedom of men to the influences of the heavenly bodies, prognosticates future events from the position of these, as contrasted with "astronomy," that true science which investigates the laws of the heavenly bodies in their relations to one another and to the planet upon which we dwell.

As these are both from the Greek, so "despair,"

and "diffidence" are both, though the second more directly than the first, from the Latin. At a period not very long past the difference between them was hardly appreciable; it certainly could not be affirmed of one that it was very much stronger than the other. If in one the absence of all *hope*, in the other that of all *faith*, was implied. In proof I would only refer you to a book with which I am sure every English schoolmaster will wish to be familiar, I mean *The Pilgrim's Progress*, where Mistress "Diffidence" is Giant "Despair's" wife, and not a whit behind him in her deadly enmity to the pilgrims; even as Jeremy Taylor speaks of the impenitent sinner's "diffidence" in the hour of death, meaning, as the context plainly shows, his despair. But to what end two words for one and the same thing? And thus "diffidence" did not retain that force of meaning which it had at the first, but little by little assumed a more mitigated sense (Hobbes speaks of "men's diffidence," that is distrust, "of one another"), till it has come in our present English to signify a becoming distrust of ourselves, an humble estimate of our own powers, with only a slight intimation in the word, that perhaps this distrust is carried too far.

Again, "interference" and "interposition" are both from the Latin; and here too it lies not by any anterior necessity in the several derivations of the words, that they should have the different shades of meaning which yet they have obtained among us: the Latin verbs which form their latter halves being about as strong one as the other. And yet in our practical use, "interference" is something offensive; it is the pushing in of himself between two parties on the part of a third, who was not asked, and is not thanked for his pains, and who, as the feeling of the word implies, had no business there; while "interposition" is employed to express the friendly peacemaking mediation of one whom the act well became, and who, even if he was not specially invited thereunto, is still thanked for what he has done. How real an increase is it in the wealth and capabilities of a language thus to have discriminated such words as these; and to be able to express acts outwardly the same by different words, as we would praise or blame them.*

But these which I have named are not the only desynonymizing processes which are going forward in a language; for we may observe in almost all lan-

* It must at the same time be acknowledged, that if in the course of time distinctions are thus created, and if this is the tendency of language, yet they are also sometimes, though far less often, obliterated. Thus the fine distinction between "yea" and "yes," "nay" and "no," that once existed in English has quite disappeared. "Yea" and "nay," in Wiclif's time, and a good deal later, were the answers to questions framed in the affirmative. "Will he come?" To this it would have been replied, "Yea" or "Nay," as the case might be. But, "Will he not come?"—to this the answer would have been, "Yes," or "No." Sir Thomas More finds fault with Tyndale, that in his translation of the Bible he had not observed this distinction, which was evidently therefore going out even then, that is in the reign of Henry VIII.; and shortly after it was quite forgotten.

guages, and not the least in our own, a tendency to the formation of new words out of what were at the first no more than different pronunciations, or even slightly different spellings, of one and the same word; which yet in the end detach themselves from one another, not again to reunite; just as accidental varieties in fruits or flowers, produced at hazard, have yet permanently separated off and settled into different kinds. Sometimes as the accent is placed on one syllable of a word or another, it comes to have different significations, and those so distinctly marked that it may be considered out of one word to have grown into two. Examples of this are the following: "dívers" and "divérse;" "cónjure" and "conjúre;" "ántic" and "antíque;" "húman" and "humáne;" "géntle" and "gentéel;" "cústom" and "custúme;" "éssay" and "assáy;" "próperty" and "propríety." Again a word is pronounced with a full sound of its syllables or more shortly: thus "spirit" and "spright;" "blossom" and "bloom;" "piety" and "pity;" "courtesy" and "curtsey;" "personality" and "personalty;" "fantasy" and "fancy;" "triumph" and "trump" (the winning card);* "happily" and "haply;" "eremite" and "hermit;" "poesy" and "posy;" or with the dropping of the first syllable: "history" and "story;" "etiquette" and "ticket;" "estate"

* If there were any doubt about this matter, which indeed there is not, a reference to Latimer's famous *Sermon on Cards* would abundantly remove it, where "triumph" and "trump" are interchangeably used.

and "state;"—or without losing a syllable, with more or less stress laid on the close: "regiment" and "regimen;" "corpse" and "corps;" "bite" and "bit;" "sire" and "sir;" "stripe" and "strip;" "borne" and "born;" "clothes" and "cloths." Or there has grown up some other slight distinction, as between "ghostly" and "ghastly;" "utter" and "outer;" "mettle" and "metal;" "parson" and "person;" "ingenious" and "ingenuous;" "prune" and "preen;" "mister" and "master;" "villain" and "villein;" "cleft" and "clift," now written "cliff;" "cure" and "care;" "travel" and "travail;" "pennon" and "pinion;" "can" and "ken;" "oaf" and "elf;" "gambol" and "gamble;" "truth" and "troth;" "quay" and "key;" "lose" and "loose;" "cant" and "chant;" "price" and "prize;" "errant" and "arrant;" "benefit" and "benefice;"* I do not know whether we ought to add to these, "news" and "noise," which some tell us to be the same word;

* Were there need of proving that these both lie in "beneficium," which there is not, for in Wiclif's translation of the Bible the distinction is still latent (1 Tim. vi. 2), one might adduce a singularly characteristic little trait of papal policy which once turned upon the double use of this word. Pope Adrian the Fourth writing to the emperor Frederic the First to complain of certain conduct of his, reminded the emperor that he had placed the imperial crown upon his head, and would willingly have conferred even greater "beneficia" upon him than this. Had the word been allowed to pass, it would no doubt have been afterward appealed to as an admission on the part of the great emperor that he held the empire as a feud or fief (for "beneficium" was then the technical word for this, though the meaning has much narrowed since), from the pope—the very point in dispute between them. The word was indignantly repelled by

at any rate the identifying of them is instructive, for how much news is but noise, and passes away like a noise before long. Or, it may be, the difference which constitutes the two forms of the word into two words is one in the spelling, and so slight a one even there as to be appreciable only by the eye, and to escape altogether the ear: thus is it with "draft" and "draught;" "plain" and "plane;" "flower" and "flour;" "check" and "cheque."

Now if you will follow up these instances, you will find, I believe, in every case that there has attached itself to the different forms of the words a modification of meaning more or less sensible, that each has won for itself an independent sphere of meaning, in which it, and it only, moves. For take a few instances in proof. "Divers" implies difference only, but "diverse" difference with opposition; thus the several evangelists narrate the same events in "divers" manners, but not in "diverse." "Antique" is ancient, but "antic" is now the ancient regarded as overlived, out of date, and so in our days grotesque, ridiculous; and then, with a dropping of the reference to age, the grotesque, the ridiculous alone. "Human" is what every man is, "humane" is what every man ought to be; for Johnson's sug-

the emperor and the whole German nation, whereupon the pope appealed to the etymology, that "beneficium" was but "bonum factum," and had the meanness to say that he meant no more than to remind the emperor of the "benefits" which he had done him, and which he would willingly multiply still more.

gestion that "humane" is from the French feminine, "humaine," and "human" from the masculine, can not for an instant be admitted. "Ingenious" is an adjective expressing a mental, "ingenuous" a moral excellence. A gardiner "prunes," that is, trims his trees, birds "preen" or trim their feathers. "Bloom" is a finer and more delicate efflorescence even than "blossom;" thus, the "bloom," but not the "blossom" of the cheek. A "curtsey" is one, and that merely an external manifestation of "courtesy." "Gambling" may be, as with a fearful irony it is called, *play*, but it is nearly as distant from "gambolling" as hell is from heaven. Nor would it be hard, in each other of the words which I have instanced, nor in others of like kind which no doubt might be added to them, to trace a distinction which has made itself more or less strongly felt.*

Let us now take some words which are not thus desynonymized by usage only, but which have an inherent etymological distinction—one, however, which it might be easy to overlook, which, so long as we dwell on the surface of the word, we shall overlook; and let us see whether we shall not be

* The same happens in other languages. Thus in Latin "pinna" and "penna" are only different spellings of the same word, and signify alike a "wing;" while yet in practice "penna" has come to be used for the wing of a bird, "pinna" (the diminutive of which, "pinnaculum," has given us "pinnacle") for that of a building. So is it with "codex" and "caudex," "infacetus" and "inficetus;" in the German with "rechtlich" and "redlich;" in French with "harnois," the armor, or "harness," of a soldier, "harnais" of a horse.

gainers by bringing out the distinction into clear consciousness. Here are the words "arrogant," "presumptuous," and "insolent." We often use them promiscuously; yet let us examine them a little more closely, and ask ourselves, as soon as we have succeeded in tracing the lines of demarcation between them, whether we are not now in possession of three distinct thoughts, instead of a single confused one. Thus, he is "arrogant," who oversteps the limits of what justly is his, claims the observance and homage of others as his due (ad rogat), does not wait for them to offer, but himself demands it; or who, having right to one sort of observance, claims another to which he has no right. Thus, it was "arrogance" in Nebuchadnezzar, when he required that all men should fall down before the image which he had reared. He, a man, was claiming for man's work the homage which belonged only to God. But one is "presumptuous" who *takes* things to himself *before* he has acquired any right and title to them (præ sumit), the young man who already takes the place of the old, the learner who speaks as with the authority of the teacher. By-and-by all this may very justly be his, but it is "presumption" to anticipate it now. "Insolent" means properly no more than unusual; to act "insolently" is to act unusually. The offensive sense which the word has acquired rests upon the feeling that there is a certain well-understood rule of society, a recognised standard of moral behavior, to which each of its members should conform. The "insolent" man is one who violates this rule, who breaks through this order, acting in an unaccustomed manner. The same sense of the orderly being also the moral, speaks out in the word "irregular;" a man of "irregular," is for us a man of immoral life; and yet more strongly in the Latin language, which has but one word (mores) for customs and morals.

Or consider the following words; "to hate," "to loathe," "to detest," and "to abhor." Each of them rests on an image entirely distinct from the others; two, that is the first and second, being Anglo-Saxon, and the others Latin. "To hate" is properly to be *inflamed* with passionate dislike, the word being connected with "heat," "hot;" just as we speak, using the same figure, of persons being "incensed" with anger, or of their anger "kindling:" "ira" and "uro" being perhaps related. "To loathe" is properly to feel nausea, the turning of the stomach at that which excites first natural, and then by a transfer, moral disgust. "To detest" is to bear witness against, not to be able to keep silence in regard of something, to feel ourselves obliged to lift up our voice and testimony against it. "To abhor" is to shrink shuddering back, as one would from an object of fear, a hissing serpent rising in one's path. Our blessed Lord "hated" to see his Father's house profaned, when, the zeal of that house consuming him, he drove forth in anger the profaners from it: he "loathed" the lukewarmness of the Laodiceans, when he threatened to reject them out of his mouth; he "detested" the hypocrisy of the Pharisees and scribes, when he proclaimed their sin and uttered those eight woes against them (Matt. 23). He "abhorred" the evil suggestions of Satan, when he bade the tempter to get behind him, seeking to put a distance between himself and him.

You will observe that in most of the words which I have adduced, I have sought to refer their usage to their etymologies, to follow the guidance of these, and by the same aid to trace the lines of demarcation which divide them. For I can not but think it an omission in a very instructive little volume upon synonyms which has lately been edited by Archbishop Whately, and a partial diminution of its usefulness, that in the valuation of words reference is so seldom made to these, the writer relying almost entirely on present usage, and the tact and instinct of a cultivated mind for the appreciation of them aright. The accomplished author (or authoress) of this book indeed justifies this omission on the ground that a book of synonyms has to do with the present relative value of words, not with their roots and derivations; and further, that a reference to these brings in often what is only a disturbing force in the process, tending to confuse rather than to clear.* But while it is

* Among the words of which the etymology, if we were to suffer

quite true that words may often ride very slackly at anchor on their etymologies, may be borne hither and thither by the shifting tides and currents of usage, yet are they for the most part still holden by them. Very few have broken away and drifted from their moorings altogether. A "novelist," or writer of *new* tales in the present day is very different from a "novelist" or upholder of *new* theories in politics and religion of two hundred years ago; yet the idea of *newness* is common to them both. A "naturalist" was then a denier of revealed truth, of any but *natural* religion; he is now an investigator and often a pious one of *nature* and of its laws; yet the word has remained true to its etymology all the

ourselves to be led by it, would place us altogether on a wrong track as to its present meaning, the writer adduces "allegiance," which by usage signifies "the fidelity of the subject to his prince," while the etymology would rather suggest "conformity to law." But surely this derivation of it, as though it were "ad legem," is an erroneous one. It is rather derived from "alligo," as "liege" from "ligo;" and thus is perfectly true to its etymology, signifying as it does the obligation wherewith one is bound to his superior. Algernon Sidney, in his *Discourse concerning Government*, c. 3, § 36, falls into the same mistake; for, replying to some who maintained that submission was due to kings, even though they should act in direct contradiction to the fundamental laws of the kingdom, he observes that the very word "allegiance," of which they made so much, refuted them; for this was plainly "such an obedience as the law requires." He would have done better appealing, as indeed on one occasion he does to the word "loyalty," which, being derived from "loi," expresses properly that fidelity which one owes according to law, and does not necessarily include that attachment to the royal person, which happily we in England have been able further to throw into the word.

while. A "methodist" was once a follower of a certain "method" of philosophical induction, now of a "method" in the fulfilment of religious duties; but in either case "method," or orderly progression, is the soul of the word. Take other words which have changed or modified their meaning—"plantations," for instance, which were once colonies of men (and indeed we still "plant" a colony), but are now nurseries of young trees, and you will find the same to hold good. "Ecstacy" *was* madness, it *is* delight, but in neither case has it departed from its fundamental meaning, since it is the nature alike of this and that *to set men out of and beside themselves.*

And even when the matter is not so obvious as in these cases, the etymology of a word exercises an unconscious influence upon its usages, oftentimes makes itself felt when least expected, so that a word, after seeming quite to have forgotten, will, after longest wanderings, return to it again. And one of the arts of a great poet or prose-writer, who wishes to add emphasis to his style, to bring out all the latent forces of his native tongue, will very often be to reconnect by his use of it, a word with its original derivation, and not suffer it to forget itself though it would. How often Milton does this.* And even if

* Yet the best example which I have at hand is one from the French, from Bossuet, who in his panegyric of the great Condé expresses himself thus: "On le vit *étonner* de ses régards étincelants ceux qui échappaient à ses coups." Take *étonner* in its ordinary secondary sense, and how feeble and pointless the whole; but doubt-

all this were not so, yet the past history of a word, which history must needs *start* from its derivation, how soon soever that may be left behind, is surely a necessary element in its present valuation. A man may be wholly different now from what once he was, yet not the less to know his antecedents is needful, before we can ever perfectly understand his present self; and the same holds good with a word.

There is often a moral value in the possession of synonyms, enabling us, as they do, to say exactly what we intend, without exaggeration or the putting of more into our words than we feel in our hearts, allowing us, as one has said, to be at once courteous and precise. Such moral advantage there is, for example, in the choice which we have between the words "to felicitate" and "to congratulate," for the expressing of our sentiments and wishes in regard of the good fortune that happens to others. "To felicitate" another is to wish him happiness, without affirming that his happiness is also ours. Thus out of that general good will with which we ought to regard all, we might "felicitate" one almost a stranger to us; nay, more, I can honestly felicitate one on his appointment to a post, or attainment of an honor, even though I may not consider him the fittest to have obtained it, though I should have been glad if another had done so; I can desire and hope, that is,

less the orator brought it back to the "attonitus" from which it and our "astonish" alike proceed, and then, how grand its employment that it may bring all joy and happiness to him. But I could not, without a violation of truth, "congratulate" him, or that stranger whose prosperity awoke no lively delight in my heart; for when I "congratulate" a person (*con gratulor*), I declare that I am sharer in his joy, that what has rejoiced him has rejoiced also me. We have all, I dare say, felt, even without having made any such analysis of the distinction between the words, that "congratulate" is a far heartier word than "felicitate," and one with which it much better becomes us to welcome the good fortune of a friend; and the analysis, as you perceive, perfectly justifies the feeling. "Felicitations" are little better than compliments; "congratulations" are the expression of a genuine sympathy and joy.

Let me illustrate the importance of synonymous distinctions by another example, by the words, "to invent" and "to discover;" "invention" and "discovery." How slight may seem to us the distinction between them, even if we see any at all. Yet try them a little closer, try them, which is true proof, by aid of examples, and you will perceive that by no means can they be indifferently used — that on the contrary a great principle lies at the root of their distinction. Thus we speak of the "invention" of printing, the "discovery" of America. Shift these words, and speak, for instance, of the "invention" of America; you feel as once how unsuitable the language is. And why? Because Columbus did not make that to be which before him had not been. America was there, before he revealed it to European eyes; but that which before was, he showed to be; he withdrew the veil which hitherto had concealed it; he "discovered" it. So, too, we speak of Newton "discovering" the law of gravity; he drew aside the veil whereby men's eyes were hindered from perceiving it, but the law had existed from the beginning of the world, and would have existed whether he or any other man had traced it or no; neither was it in any way affected by the discovery of it which he had made. But Guttemburg, or whoever else it may have been to whom the honor belongs, "invented" printing; he made something to be, which hitherto was not. In like manner Harvey "discovered" the circulation of the blood; but Watt "invented" the steam-engine; and we speak with a true distinction of the "inventions" of art, the "discoveries" of science. In the very highest matters of all, it is deeply important that we be aware of and observe the distinction. In religion there have been many "discoveries" but (in true religion I mean), no "inventions." Many discoveries—but God in each case is the discoverer; he draws away the veils, one veil after another, that have hidden him from men; the discovery or revelation is from himself, for no man by searching has found out God; and, therefore, wherever anything offers itself as an "invention" in matters of religion, it proclaims itself a lie—all self-devised worships, all religions which man projects from his own heart. Just that is known of God which he is pleased to make known, and no more; and men's recognising or refusing to recognise in nowise affects it. They may deny or own him, but he continues the same.

As involving in like manner a distinction which can not safely be lost sight of, how important is it to keep in mind the difference, of which the existence is asserted by the fact that we possess the two words, "to apprehend" and "to comprehend," with their substantives, "apprehension" and "comprehension." For indeed we "apprehend" many truths, which we do not "comprehend." The great mysteries of our faith, the doctrine for instance of the Holy Trinity —we lay hold upon it (*ad prehendo*), we hang on it, our souls live by it; but we do not "comprehend" it, that is, we do not take it all in; for it is a necessary attribute of God that he is incomprehensible; if he were not so, he would not be God, or the being that comprehended him would be God also. But it also belongs to the idea of God that he may be "apprehended," though not "comprehended," by his reasonable creatures; he has made them to know him, though not to know him all, to "apprehend," though not to "comprehend" him. We may transfer with profit the same distinction to matters not quite so solemn. I read Goldsmith's *Trav-*

eller, or one of Gay's fables, and I feel that I "comprehend" it. I do not believe, that is, that there was anything in the poet's mind or intention, which I have not in the reading reproduced in my own. But I read *Hamlet*, or *King Lear:* here I "apprehend" much; I have wondrous glimpses of the poet's intention and aim; but I do not for an instant suppose that I have "comprehended," taken in, that is, all that was in his mind in the writing; or that his purpose does not stretch in manifold directions far beyond the range of my vision; and I am sure there are few who would not shrink from affirming, at least if they at all realized the force of the words they were using, that they "comprehended" Shakspere; however much they may "apprehend" in him.

How often "opposite" and "contrary" are used as if there was no difference between them, and yet there is a most essential one, one which perhaps we may best express by saying that "opposites" *complete*, while "contraries" *exclude* one another. Thus the most "opposite" moral or mental characteristics may meet in one and the same person, while to say that the most "contrary" did so, would be manifestly absurd; for example, a man may be at once prudent and bold, for these are opposites; he could not be at once prudent and rash, for these are contraries. We may love and fear at the same time and the same person; we pray in the litany that we may love and fear God, the two being opposites and thus the complements of one another; but to pray that we might love and hate would be as absurd as it would be impious, for these are contraries, and could no more co-exist together than white and black, hot and cold, at the same time in the same subject; or, to take another illustration, sweet and sour are "opposites," sweet and bitter are "contraries."* It will be seen then that there is always a certain relation between opposites; they unfold themselves though in different directions from the same root, as the positive and negative forces of electricity, and in their very opposition uphold and sustain one another; while contraries encounter one another from quarters diverse, and one only subsists in the exact degree that it puts out of working the other. Surely this distinction can not be an unimportant one either in the region of ethics or elsewhere.

It will happen continually that rightly to distinguish between two words will throw great light upon some controversy in which those words play a principal part, nay, will virtually put an end to that controversy altogether. Thus when Hobbes, with a true instinct, would have laid deep the foundations of atheism and despotism together, resolving all right into might, and taking away from men, if he could, not merely the power, but denying to them the duty of obeying God rather than man, his moral sophisms

* See Coleridge's *Church and State*, p. 18.

could stand only so long as it was not perceived that "compulsion" and "obligation," with which he juggled, conveyed two ideas perfectly distinct, indeed disparate, in kind, and that what pertained to one had been transferred to the other by a mere confusion of terms and cunning sleight of hand, the one being a physical, the other a moral necessity. There is indeed no such fruitful source of confusion and mischief as this — to words are tacitly assumed as equivalent, and therefore exchangeable, and then that which may be assumed, and with truth, of one, is assumed also of the other, of which it is not true. Thus, for instance, it often is with "instruction" and "education." Can not we "instruct" a child, it is asked, can not we teach it geography, or arithmetic, or grammar, quite independently of the catechism, or even of the Scriptures? No doubt you may, but can you "educate," without bringing moral and spiritual forces to bear upon the mind and affections of the child? And you must not be permitted to transfer the admissions which we freely make in regard of "instruction," as though they also held good in respect of "education." For what is "education"? Is it a furnishing of a man from without with knowledge and facts and information? or is it a drawing forth from within and a training of the spirit, of the true humanity which is latent within him? Is the process of education the filling of the child's mind, as a cistern is filled with waters brought in buckets from some other source, or the opening up of its own fountains? Now if we give any heed to the word "education," and to the voice which speaks in the word, we shall not long be in doubt. Education must educe, being from "educare," which is but another form of "educere;" and that is "to draw out," and not "to put in." "To draw out" what is in the child, the immortal spirit which is there, this is the end of education; and so much the word declares. The putting in is indeed most needful, that is, the child must be instructed as well as educated, and the word "instruction" just means furnishing; but not instructed instead of educated. He must first have powers awakened in him, measures of spiritual value given him; and then he will know how to deal with the facts of this outward world; then instruction in these will profit him; but not without the higher training, still less as a substitute for it.

It has occasionally happened that the question of which out of two apparent synonyms should be adopted in some important state document has been debated with no little earnestness and vigor. Thus was it, for example, at the great English revolution of 1688, when the two houses of parliament were for a considerable time at issue whether it should be declared of James the Second, that he had "abdicated," or "deserted," the throne. This might seem at first sight a mere strife about words, and yet, in reality, serious constitutional questions were involved in the selection of the one word or the other. The commons insisted on the word "abdicated," not as wishing to imply that in any act of the late king there had been an official renunciation of the crown, which would have been manifestly untrue; but because "abdicated" to their minds alone expressed the fact that James had so borne himself as virtually to have entirely renounced, disowned, and relinquished the crown, to have irrevocably forfeited and separated himself from it, and from any right to it for ever; while "deserted" would have seemed to leave room and an opening for a return, which they were determined to declare for ever excluded; as, were it said of a husband that he had "deserted" his wife, or of a soldier that he had "deserted" his colors, this language would imply not only that he might, but that he ought and was bound to return. Lord Somers' speech on the occasion is a masterly specimen of synonymous discrimination, and an evidence of the uses in highest matters of state to which it may be turned.

Let me press upon you in conclusion some few of the many advantages to be derived from the habit of distinguishing synonyms. These advantages we might presume to be many, even though we could not ourselves perceive them; for how often do the great masters of style in every tongue, perhaps none so often as Cicero, the greatest of all,* pause to discriminate between the words they are using; how much care and labor, how much subtlety of thought, they have counted well bestowed on the operation; how much importance do they avowedly attach to it; not to say that their works, even where they do not intend it, will be a continual lesson in this respect a great writer merely in the accuracy with which he employs words will always be exercising us in synonymous discrimination. But the advantages of attending to them need not be taken on trust; they are evident. How great a part of true wisdom it is to be able to distinguish between things that differ, things seemingly, but not really alike, this is remarkably attested by our words "discernment" and "discretion;" which are now used as equivalent, the first to "insight," the second to "prudence;" while yet in their earlier usage, and according to their etymology, being both from "discerno," they signify

* Thus he distinguishes between voluntas and cupiditas; cautio and metus (*Tusc.* 4, 6); gaudium, lætitia, voluptas (*Tusc.* 4, 6; *Fin.* 2, 4); caritas and amor (*De Part. Or.* 25); ebrius and ebriosus, iracundus and iratus, anxietas and angor (*Tusc.* 4, 12); vitium, morbus, ægrotatio (*Tusc.* 4, 13); labor and dolor (*Tusc.* 2, 15); malitia and vitiositas (*Tusc.* 4, 15); Quintilian also often bestows attention on synonyms, observing well (vi. 3, 17): "Pluribus nominibus in eâdem re vulgo utimur; quæ tamen si diducas, suam quandam propriam vim ostendent:" and among church writers, Augustine is a frequent and mostly a successful discriminator of words. Thus he separates off from one another flagitium and facinus (*De Doct. Christ.* 3, 10); æmulatio and invidia (*Exp. ad Gal.* v. 20); arrha and pignus (*Serm.* 23, 8, 9); with many more.

the power of so seeing things that in the seeing we distinguish and separate them one from another. Such were originally "discernment" and "discretion," and such in great measure they are still. And in words is a material ever at hand on which to train the spirit to a skilfulness in this; on which to exercise its sagacity through the habit of distinguishing there where it would be so easy to confound. Nor is this habit of discrimination only valuable as a part of our intellectual training; but what a positive increase is it of mental wealth when we have learned to discern between things, which really differ, but have been hitherto confused in our minds; and have made these distinctions permanently our own in the only way by which they can be made secure, that is, by assigning to each its appropriate word and peculiar sign.

What a help moreover will it prove to the writing of a good English style, if instead of having many words before us, and choosing almost at random and at hap-hazard from among them, we at once know which, and which only, we ought in the case before us to employ, which will be the exact vesture of our thoughts. It is the first characteristic of a well-dressed man that his clothes fit him: they are not too small and shrunken here, too large and loose there. Now it is precisely such a prime characteristic of a good style that the words fit close to the thoughts: they will not be too big here, hanging like a giant's robe on the limbs of a dwarf; nor too small there, as a boy's garments into which the man has with difficulty and ridiculously thrust himself. You do not feel in one place that the writer means more than he has succeeded in saying; in another that he has said more than he means; or in a third something beside what his intention was: and all this, from a lack of dexterity in employing the instrument of language, of precision in knowing what words would be the exactest correspondents and fittest exponents of his thought.

Now let us suppose this power of exactly saying what we mean, and neither more nor less than we mean, to be merely an elegant mental accomplishment. It is indeed this, and perhaps there is no power so surely indicative of a high and accurate training of the intellectual faculties. But it is also much more than this: it has a moral meaning as well. It is nearly allied to morality, inasmuch as it is nearly connected with truthfulness. Every man who has himself in any degree cared for the truth, and occupied himself in seeking it, is more or less aware how much of the falsehood in the world passes current under the concealment of words, how many strifes and controversies,

"Which feed the simple, and offend the wise,"

find all or nearly all their fuel and their nourishment in words carelessly or dishonestly employed. And when a man has had any actual experience of this fact, and has at all perceived how far this mischief reaches, he is sometimes almost tempted to say with Shakspere's clown, "Words are grown so false, I am loath to prove reason with them." He can not, however, forego their employment, not to say that he will presently perceive that this falseness of theirs whereof he accuses them, this cheating power of words, is not of their proper use, but their abuse; that however they may have been enlisted in the service of lies, they are yet of themselves most true, and that where the bane is, there the antidote should be sought as well. Ask then words what they mean, that you may deliver yourselves, that you may help to deliver others from the tyranny of words, and from the strife of "word-warriors." Learn to distinguish between them, for you have the authority of Hooker, that "the mixture of those things by speech, which by nature are divided, is the mother of all error." And although I can not promise you that the study of synonyms, or the acquaintance with derivations, or any other knowledge but the very highest knowledge of all, will deliver you from the temptation to misuse this or any other gift of God — a temptation which always lies so near us — yet I am sure that these studies rightly pursued will do much in leading us to stand in awe of this divine gift of words, and to tremble at the thought of turning it to any other than those worthy ends for which God has endowed us with it.

LECTURE VI.

THE SCHOOLMASTER'S USE OF WORDS.

I SHALL now attempt to apply, and to suggest some ways in which you may apply, what has been hitherto spoken to practical ends, and make this study of words, which I have been pressing upon you, to tell upon your own teaching hereafter; for assuredly we ought never to disconnect what we ourselves may learn, from the hope and expectation of being able by its aid to teach others more effectually; our studies, when we do so, become instantly a selfish thing. There is a noble line in Chaucer, where, characterizing the true scholar, he says of him,

"And gladly would he learn, and gladly teach,"

and in the spirit of this line I trust that we shall each one of us work and live.

But to address ourselves to the matter more directly in hand. You all here are made acquainted with a good deal more than the first rudiments of the Latin tongue. Every one who can at all appreciate what your future task will be, must rejoice that it is so. Indeed, it is hard to understand how you could be otherwise fitted and accomplished for the work which you have before you. It is conceivable in languages like the Greek and the German, which, for all practical purposes, may be considered rounded and complete in themselves, which contain all the resources for discovering the origin and meaning of their words in their own bosom, or so nearly so, that the few exceptions need not be taken into account, in such languages, I say, it is conceivable that a thorough knowledge of his own tongue may be attained by one who remains ignorant of any other, and that himself possessing, he may be able to impart this same knowledge to others. In fact, the Greek, who certainly understood his own language thoroughly, never did extend his knowledge beyond it. But it is different with English. Would we follow up its words, not to their remotest sources, but only a step or two, it carries us at once beyond itself and to a foreign soil, and mainly to the Latin. This being the case, he who has not some acquaintance with Latin can only explain a vast number of words loosely and at hazard; he has some general sense or impression of what they intend, of the ideas which they represent, but nothing certain. He stands on no solid ground; he does not feel able to plant himself securely as at a middle point, from which, as from a common centre, all its different meanings diverge.

And having these convictions in regard of the advantage of following up words to their sources of "deriving" them, that is, of tracing each little rill to the river from which it first was drawn, let me here observe, as something not remote from our subject, but, on the contrary, directly bearing upon it, that I can conceive no method of so effectually defacing and barbarizing our English tongue, no scheme that would go so far to empty it, practically at least and for us, of all the hoarded wit, wisdom, imagination, and history which it contains, to cut the vital nerve which connects its present with the past, as the introduction of the scheme of "phonetic spelling," which some have lately been zealously advocating among us; the principle of which is that all words should be spelt according as they are sounded, that the writing should be, in every case, subordinated to the speaking.

The tacit assumption that it ought so to be is the pervading error running through the whole system. But there is no necessity that it should; every word on the contrary has *two* existences, as a spoken word and a written; and you have no right to sacrifice one of these, or even to subordinate it wholly, to the other. A word exists as truly for the eye as for the ear, and in a highly advanced state of society, where reading is almost as universal as speaking, as much perhaps for the first as for the last. That in the *written* word moreover is the permanence and continuity of language and of learning, and that the connection is most intimate of a true orthography with all this, is affirmed in our words "letters," "literature," "unlettered," even as in other languages by words entirely corresponding to these.*

The gains consequent on the introduction of such a change as is proposed would be insignificantly small, while the losses would be enormously great. The gains would be the saving of a certain amount of labor in the learning to spell; an amount of labor, however, absurdly exaggerated by the promoters of the scheme. This labor, whatever it is, would be in great part saved, as the pronunciation would at once put in possession of the spelling; if, indeed, spelling or orthography could then be said to exist. But even this insignificant gain would not long remain, seeing that pronunciation is itself continually altering; custom is lord here for better or for worse; and a multitude of words are now pronounced in a different manner from that of a hundred years ago, so that, ere very long, there would again be a chasm between the spelling and pronunciation of words; — unless indeed the former were to vary, as I do not see well how it could consistently refuse to do with each variation of the latter, reproducing each one of its barbarous or capricious alterations; which thus it must be remembered, would be changes not in the pronunciation only, but in the word itself, for the word would only exist as a pronounced word, the written being a mere shadow of this. When these had multiplied a little, and they would indeed multiply ex-

* As *litteræ*, *γράμματα*, *ἀγράμματος*.

ceedingly, so soon as the barrier against them which now exists was removed, what the language would ere long become, it is not easy to guess.

This fact, however, though alone sufficient to show how little the scheme of phonetic spelling would remove even those inconveniences which it proposes to remedy, is only the smallest objection to it. The far deeper and more serious one is, that in innumerable instances, it would obliterate altogether those clear marks of birth and parentage, which, if not all, yet so many of our words bear now upon their very fronts, or are ready, upon a very slight interrogation, to declare to us. Words have now an ancestry; and the ancestry of words as of men is often a very noble part of them, making them capable of great things, because those from whom they are descended have done great things before them; but this would deface their scutcheon, and bring them all to the same ignoble level. Words are now a nation, grouped into tribes and families, some smaller, some larger; this change would go far to reduce them to a promiscuous and barbarous horde. Now they are often translucent with their idea, as an alabaster vase is lighted up by a lamp placed within it; in how many cases would this inner light be then quenched. They have now a body and a soul, and the soul looking through the body; oftentimes then nothing but the body, not seldom nothing but the carcase, of the word would remain. Both these objections were urged long ago by Bacon, who characterizes this so-called reformation, "that writing should be consonant to speaking," as "a branch of unprofitable subtlety;" and especially urges that thereby "the derivations of words, especially from foreign languages are utterly defaced and extinguished."

From the results of various approximations to phonetic spelling, which from time to time have been made, and the losses which have thereon ensued, we may guess what the loss would be were the system fully carried out. When "fancy" was spelt "phantsy," as by Sylvester in his translation of Du Bartas, and by the other scholarlike writers of that time, no one could then doubt of its connection, or rather its original identity, with "phantasy," as no Greek scholar could miss its relation with φαντασία. Of those sufficiently acquainted with Latin, it would be curious to know how many have seen "silva" in "savage," since it has been so written, and not "salvage," as of old? or have been reminded of the hinderances to a civilized state of existence which the indomitable forest, more perhaps than any other obstacle, presents. Spell "analyse" as I have sometimes seen it, and as phonetically it ought to be, "analize," and the tap-root of the word is cut. What number of readers will recognise in it then the image of dissolving and resolving aught into its elements, and use it with a more or less conscious reference to this? It may be urged that few do so even now among those who employ the word. The more need they should not be fewer; for these few do in fact retain the word in its place, prevent it from gradually drifting from it, preserve its vitality not merely for themselves, but also for the others that have not this knowledge. In phonetic spelling is in fact the proposal that the educated should voluntarily place themselves in the conditions and under the disadvantages of the ignorant and uneducated, instead of seeking to elevate these last to theirs.*

Even now the relationship of words, which are so important for our right understanding of them, are continually overlooked; a very little thing serving to conceal them from us. For example, what a multitude of our nouns substantive and adjective are, in fact, unsuspected participles, or are otherwise most

* The same attempt to introduce phonetic spelling, or "phonography" as it is there called, has been several times made, once in the sixteenth century, and again some twenty years ago, in France. Let us see by one or two examples what would be the results there. Here is the word "temps;" from which the phronographists omit the *p* as superfluous. What is the consequence? at once its visible connection with the Latin "tempus," with the Spanish "tiempo," with the Italian "tempo," with its own "temporel" and "temporaire," is broken, and for many effaced. Or again, here are "poids" a weight, "poix" pitch, "pois" peas. I do not suppose the Frenchman who spoke his own language the best, could mark in pronunciation the distinction between these; and thus to the ear there may be confusion between them, but to the eye there is none; not to say that the *d* in "poids" puts it for us at once in relation with "pondus," the *x* in "poix" with "pix," the *s* in "pois" with the low Latin "pisum." In each case the letter which these improvers of orthography would dismiss as useless and worse than useless, contains the secret of the word.

closely connected with verbs, with which, notwithstanding, until some one points out the fact to us, we probably never think of putting them in any relation. And yet with how lively an interest shall we discover words to be of closest kin, which we had never considered till now, but as entire strangers to one another; what a real increase will it be in our acquaintance with, and mastery of, English to become aware of such relationship. Thus "heaven" is only the perfect of "to heave;" and is so called because it is "heaved" or "heaven" up, being properly the sky as it is raised aloft; the "smith" has his name from the sturdy blows that he "smites" upon the anvil; "wrong" is the perfect participle of "to wring," that which one has "wrung" or wrested from the right; just as in French "tort," from "torqueo," is that which is twisted; "guilt" of "to guile" or "beguile;" to find "guilt" in a man is to find that he has been "beguiled," that is by the devil, "instigante diabolo," as it is inserted in all indictments for murder, the forms of which come down to us from a time when men were not ashamed of tracing evil to his inspiration. The "brunt" of the battle is the "heat" of the battle, where it "burns" the most fiercely. "Haft," as of a knife, is properly only the participle perfect of "to have," that whereby you "have" or hold it. Or take two or three nouns adjective; "strong" is the participle past of "to string;" a "strong" man means no more than one whose sinews are firmly "strung." The "left" hand, as distinguished from the right, is the hand which we "leave;" inasmuch as for twenty times we use the right hand, we do not once employ *it;* and it obtains its name from being "left" unused so often. "Odd" is, I believe, properly "owed;" an "odd" glove, or an "odd" shoe is one that is "owed" to another, or to which another is "owed," for the making of a pair—just as we speak of a man being "singular," wanting, that is, his match. "Wild" is the participle past of "to will;" a "wild" horse is a "willed" or self-willed horse, one that has been never tamed or taught to submit its will to the will of another; and so with a man.

This exercise of putting words in their true relation and connection with one another might be carried much further. We might take whole groups of words, which seem to us at first sight to acknowledge hardly any kinship, if indeed any, with one another, and yet with no great difficulty show that they had a common parentage and descent. For instance, here are "shire," "shore," "share," "sheers;" "shred," "sherd;" they all are derived from one Anglo-Saxon word, which signifies to separate or divide, and still exists with us in the shape of "to sheer," which made once the three perfects, "shore," "share," "shered." "Shire" is a district in England, as it is separated from the rest; a "share" is a portion of anything thus divided off; "sheers" are instruments effecting this process of separation; the "shore" is the place where the continuity of the land is interrupted or separated by the sea; a "shred" is that which is "shered" or shorn from the main piece; a "sherd" as a pot-"sherd" that which is broken off and thus divided from the vessel; and these which I have adduced by no means exhaust this group or family of words, though it would take more time than I can spare to put some other words in relation with it.

But this analyzing of groups of words for the detecting of the bond of relationship between them, and the one root out of which they all grow, is a process which may require more etymological knowledge than you possess, and more helps from books than you can always expect to command. There is another process, and one which may prove no less useful to yourselves and to others, which will lie more certainly within your reach. It will often happen that you will meet in books, sometimes in the same book, and perhaps in the same page of this book, a word used in senses so far apart from one another, that it will seem to you at first sight almost absurd to assume as possible that there can be any bond of connection between them. Now when you do thus fall in with a word employed in these two or more senses seemingly far removed from one another, accustom yourselves to seek out the bond which there certainly is between these its several uses. This tracing of that which is common to and connects all its meanings can of course only be done by getting to its heart, to the seminal meaning, from which, as from a fruitful seed, all the others unfold themselves; to the first link in the chain, from which every later one, in a direct line or a lateral, depends. And we may proceed in this investigation, certain that we shall find such, or at least that such there is to be found. For this we may start with, as being lifted above all doubt (and the non-recognition of it is *the* great fault in Johnson's dictionary), that a word has originally but one meaning, and that all the others, however widely they may diverge from one another and seem to recede from this one, may yet be affiliated upon it, may be brought back to the one central meaning, which grasps and knits them all together; just as the races of men, black, white, and red, despite of all their present diversity and dispersion, have a central point of unity in their first parents.

Let me illustrate what I mean by two or three familiar examples. Here is the word "post;" how various are the senses in which it is employed; "post"-office; "post"-haste; a "post" standing in the ground; a military "post;" an official "post;" "to post" a leger. Might one not at first presume it impossible to bring all these uses of "post" to a common centre? Yet indeed when once on the right track, nothing is easier; "post" is the Latin "positus," that which is *placed;* the piece of timber is "placed" in the ground, and so a "post;" a military station is a "post," for a man is "placed" in it, and must not quit it without orders; to travel "post," is to have certain relays of horses "placed" at intervals, that so no delay on the road may occur; the "post"-office is that which avails itself of this mode of communication; to "post" a leger is to "place" or register its several items.

Or take the word "stock;" in what an almost infinite number of senses it is employed; we have live "stock," "stock" in trade, the village "stocks," the "stock" of a gun, the "stock" dove, the "stocks" on which ships are built, the "stock" which goes round the neck, the family "stock," the "stocks," or public funds, in which money is invested, and other "stocks" very likely besides these. What point in common can we find between them all? This, that they are all derived from, and were originally the past participle of "to stick," which as it now makes "stuck," made formerly "stock;" and they cohere in the idea of *fixedness*, which is common to every one. Thus, the "stock" of a gun is that in which the barrel is fixed; the village "stocks" are those in which the feet are fastened; the "stock" in trade is the fixed capital; and so, too, the "stock" on the farm, although the fixed capital has there taken the shape of horses and cattle; in the "stocks," or public funds, money sticks fast, inasmuch as those who place it there can not withdraw or demand the capital, but receive only the interest; the "stock" of a tree is fast set in the ground; and from this use of the word it is transferred to a family; the "stock" or "stirps" is that from which it grows, and out of which it unfolds itself. And here we may bring in the "stock"-dove, as being the "stock" or stirps of the domestic kinds. I might group with these, "stake" in both its spellings; a "stake" in the hedge is stuck and fixed there; the "stakes" which men wager against the issue of a race are paid down, and thus fixed or deposited to answer the event; a beef-"steak" is a piece of meat so small that it can be stuck on the point of a fork; with much more of the same kind.

How often does the word "quick" in the creed perplex children; and even after they have learned that "the *quick* and the dead" mean the *living* and the dead, they know it only on trust; for they fail to put this "quick" in any connection with the "quick" of their own vocabulary, the "quick" with which they bid one another to throw up the ball, or the "quick"-set hedge which runs round their father's garden, or the "quick" parts for which some unwise person has praised one of them at school: yet that all these are one and the same "quick" it is of course very easy to show. Life is the fundamental idea of the word "quick," and in this its primary sense it is used in the creed, "the quick and the dead:" so too the "quick"-set hedge is properly the *living* fence, as contrasted with those made of dead timbers. But motion, as it is at once of the essence, so it is also one of the most obvious signs of life; and thus "quick" in a secondary sense was applied to all which was rapid or prompt in its motions, whether bodily or mental; thus a "quick" runner, a boy of "quick" parts; and so too "quick"-silver, and "quick" or fast shifting sands. The same sense of the connection between life and motion has given us our secondary use of the words, "animated" and "lively."

Sometimes a slightly-different spelling comes in aid of an enormous divergence of meaning, to disguise the fact of two words having originally rested on one and the same etymology, and really being so closely related to one another, that we may say, in fact, they are one and the same word. I would instance as a notable example of this, "canon" with a single *n*, as the "canon" of scripture, and "cannon," or heavy artillery. Can there, it may well be asked, be any point in common between them? can they be resolved ultimately into the same word? I believe they can. The word "canon" with the single *n*, which is a Greek word, means properly "rule;" first, the measuring rule or line of the carpenter; and then figuratively any measure or rule by which we try other things; and in its crowning use, the Holy Scriptures, as being *regulative* of life and doctrine in the church. But the carpenter's rule was commonly a reed (canna), that being selected on account of its straightness; you may remember in scripture mention once or twice being made of the measuring "reed" (Rev. xxi. 15, 16); and from this reed or "canna," the rule or line (the "canon") had its name, or at any rate the words are most closely allied. A reed, however, as we all know, besides being *straight* is also *hollow*, and thus it came to pass when the hollow engines of war, our modern artillery, were invented, and were feeling about for their appropriate name, none was nearer at hand than this which the reed supplied, and they were called "cannon" too.*

When it is thus said that we can always reduce the different meanings in which a word is employed to some one point from which they all immediately or mediately proceed, that no word has primarily more than one meaning, it must be remembered that it is quite possible there may be two words pronounced and even spelled exactly alike, which yet are wholly different in their derivation and primary usage; and that of course between these no bond of union on the score of this identity is to be sought; neither does this fact in the least invalidate the assertion. We have in such cases, as Cobbett has ex-

* In confirmation of this view of the derivation of "cannon," and in proof that it lay very near to the imagination of men to liken them to reeds, we have the application of "Rohr" in German, which, at first signifying a cane or reed, has in like manner been applied to the barrel of a gun.

pressed it well, the same combination of letters, but not the same word. Thus we have "page," one side of a leaf, from "pagina," and "page," a youthful attendant, from quite another word; "league," a treaty, from "ligare," to bind, and "league," a measure of distance, thought to be a word of Gallic origin; we have "host," an army, from "hostis," and "host," in the Roman catholic sacrifice of the mass, from "hostia;" so, too, "stories," which we tell, and "stories" or "stayeries" of a house, which we mount; "Mosaic," as the "Mosaic" law, derived from the name of the great lawgiver of Israel, "mosaic," as "mosaic work," which is "opus *musivum*;" with other words, such as "date," "mint," "ounce," "dole," "bull," "plain," not a few. In all these the identity is merely on the surface, and it would of course be lost labor to seek for a point of contact between meanings which have not any closer connection really than apparently with one another.

Let me suggest some further exercises in this region of words, which I will venture to promise that you will find profitable as ministering to the activity of your own minds, as helping to call out a like activity in those of others. Do not, I would say then once more, suffer words to pass you by, which at once provoke and promise to reward inquiry, by the readiness with which evidently they will yield up the secret of their birth or of their use, if duly interrogated by us. Many we must all be content to leave, whi h will defy all efforts to dissipate the mystery which hangs over them, but of many also it is evident on their surface that these explanations can not be very far to seek. I would instance such a word as "candidate." At a contested election how familiar are the ears of all with this word, nor can it be said to be strange to us at other times. Now does it not argue an incurious spirit to be content that this word should thus be given and received by us a hundred times, and we never to ask ourselves, What does it mean? Why is one seeking to be elected to a seat in parliament, or otherwise offering himself to the choice of his fellows, called a "candidate"? If the word lay evidently beyond our reach, we might acquiesce in our ignorance here, as in such infinite other matters; but resting, as on the face of it it does, upon the Latin "candidus," it challenges inquiry, and a very little of this would at once put us in possession of the Roman custom out of which the word grew, and to which it alludes — namely, that those who intended to offer themselves to the suffrages of the people for any of the great offices of the state, presented themselves beforehand to them in a *white* toga, being called therefore "candidati," with other not uninteresting particulars. And as it so often happens that in the act of seeking information on one subject we obtain it upon another, so will it probably be here; for in making yourself fully aware of what this custom was, you will hardly fail to learn the original meaning of "ambition," and whence we have obtained the word.

Or, again, any one who knows so much as that "verbum" means a "word," might well be struck by the fact, and if he followed it up would be led far into the relation of the parts of speech to one another, that grammarians do not employ "verbum," as one might previously have expected, to signify any word whatsoever, but restrict it to the verb alone; "verbum" is the verb. Surely here is matter for thought; why does the verb monopolize the dignity of being the "word"? what is there in it which gives it the right to do so? Is it because the verb is the animating power, the vital principle of every sentence, and that without which, either understood or uttered, no sentence can exist? or is there any other cause? I leave this to your own consideration.

Again, here is "conscience," a solemn word, if there be such in the world. Now there is not one of us whose Latin will not bring him so far as to tell him that this word is from "con" and "scire." But what does that "con" intend? "Conscience" is not merely that which I know, but that which I know *with some one else;* for this prefix can not, as I think, be esteemed superfluous, or taken to imply merely that which I know *with or to myself*. That other knower whom the word implies is God, his law making itself known and felt in the heart; and the work of "conscience" is the bringing of each of our acts and thoughts as a lesser, to be tried and measured by this as a greater, the word growing out of and declaring that awful duplicity of our moral being which arises from the presence of God in the soul—our thoughts by the standard which that presence supplies, and as the result of a comparison with it, "accusing or excusing one another."*

Once more, you call certain books "classics." You have indeed a double use of the word, for you speak of Greek and Latin as the classical languages, and the great writers in these as "*the* classics;" while at other times you hear of a "classical" English style, or of English "classics." Now "classic" is connected plainly, as we all perceive, with "classis." What then does it mean in itself, and how has it arrived at this double use? "The term is

* Many ethical writers, as is well known, pass by the "con" in their explanation of "conscience," finding merely the expression of the *certainty* of the inner moral conviction in the word; for which view they sometimes adduce the German "gewissen;" yet I can not think but that herein they err: "conscience," in the words of South, "according to the very notation of it, importing a double or joint knowledge; to wit, one of a divine law or rule, and the other of a man's own action; and so is properly the application of a general law to a particular instance of practice. And Vossius (*De Theol. Gent.* 3, 42): "Est enim conscientia syllogismus, cujus major est principium practicum à conscientiâ suggestum; minor est bona, malave actio nostra; conclusio autem actionem ad normam istius principii collatam, aut probat, aut improbat; ex quo, pro conclusionis diversitate, vel tranquilitas animi sequitur, vel intranquillitas."

drawn from the political economy of Rome. Such a man was rated as to his income in the third class, such another in the fourth, and so on; but he who was in the highest was emphatically said to be of *the* class, 'classicus'—a class-man, without adding the number, as in that case superfluous; while all others were infra classem. Hence, by an obvious analogy, the best authors were rated as 'classici,' or men of the highest class; just as in English we say 'men of rank,' absolutely for men who are in the highest ranks of the state." The mental process by which this title, which would apply rightly to the best authors in all languages, came to be often confined to those only in two, and those two to be claimed, to the seeming exclusion of all others, as *the* classical languages, is one of the most constantly recurring, and most widely extended, making itself felt in all times and in all regions of human life, and one to which I would in passing just direct your attention, though I can not here do more.

But seek, I would further urge you, to attain a consciousness of the multitude of words which there are, that now use only in a figurative sense, did yet originally rest on some fact of the outward world, vividly presenting itself to the imagination; a fact which the word has incorporated for ever, having become, as all words originally were, the indestructible vesture of a thought. If I may judge from my own experience, I think there are few intelligent boys in your schools, who would not feel that they had gotten something, when you had shown them that "to insult" means properly to leap as on the prostrate body of a foe; "to affront," to strike him on the face; that "to succor" means to run and place oneself under one that is falling, and thus support and sustain him; "to relent" (connected with "lentus," not "lenis"), to slacken the swiftness of one's pursuit; "to reprehend," to lay hold of one with the intention of forcibly pulling him back from the way of his error; that "to be examined" means to be weighed. They would be pleased to learn that a man is called "supercilious," because haughtiness with contempt of others expresses itself by the raising of the eyebrows or "supercilium;" that "subtle" is literally "fine-spun;"* that "imbecile," which we use for weak, and now always for weak in intellect, means strictly (unless indeed we must renounce this etymology), leaning upon a staff (in bacillo), as one aged or infirm might do; that "chaste" is properly white, "castus" being the participle of "candeo," as is now generally allowed; that "astonished" means struck with thunder; that "sincere" may be, I will not say that it is, without wax (*sine cerâ*), as the best and finest honey should be; that a "companion" is one with whom we share our bread, a messmate; that "desultory," which perhaps they have been warned they should not be in their

* Subtilis = subtexilis.

studies, but have never attached any very definite meaning to the warning, means properly leaping as a rider in the circus does from the back of one running horse to the back of another, this rider being technically called a "desultor;" and the word being transferred from him to those who suddenly and abruptly change their courses of study.

"Trivial," again, is a word borrowed from the life; mark three or four persons standing idly at the point where one street bisects at right angles another, and discussing there the worthless gossip, the idle nothings of the day; there you have the living explanation of the words "trivial," "trivialities," such as no explanation which did not thus root itself in the etymology would ever give you, or enable you to give to others. For there you have the "tres viæ," the "trivium;" and "trivialities" properly mean such talk as is holden by those idle loiterers that gather at these meetings of three roads. And "rivals" by curious steps has attained its present meaning; the history of which steps can hardly fail to interest. "Rivals," in the primary sense of the word, are those who dwell on the banks of the same stream. But since, as all experience shows, there is no such fruitful source of contention as a water-right, it would continually happen that these occupants of the opposite banks would be at strife with one another in regard of the periods during which they severally had a right to the use of the stream, turning it off into their own fields before the time, or leaving open the sluices beyond the time, or in other ways interfering, or being counted to interfere, with the rights of their opposite neighbors. And thus "rivals," which at first applied only to those dwellers on opposite banks of a river, came afterward to be used of any who were on any grounds in more or less unfriendly competition with one another.

Or if your future pupils shall be your companions in your walks (as it always speaks well for a teacher's influence that he is sought, not shunned by his pupils in play hours), how much will there be which you may profitably impart to them, suggested by the names of common things which will meet you there; how much which you, if you know it, will love to tell, and they will be well pleased to hear. Who would not care, for instance, to know something about the names of our English birds; that the "king-fisher," which attracted all eyes as it darted swiftly by the river's edge, was so called from the *royal* beauty, the *kingly* splendor of its plumage; that the "hawk," if it be not the same word with "havoc" (and it was called "hafoc" in Anglo-Saxon), has at least a common origin; its very name announcing the "havoc" and destruction which it makes among the smaller birds, just as in the "raven's" name is expressed its greedy, or as we say "ravenous," disposition? Or when they are listening of an evening to the harsh shriekings of the "owl," that the name of this dissonant night-bird is in fact the past participle of "to yell," and differs from "howl" in nothing but its spelling, as plainly comes out in the fact that the diminutive is as often spelt with an *h* as without it—"howlets" as often as "owlets"? Even the little "dabchick" which so haunts our waters here, diving and dipping when any one approaches, it may be as well to know why it has this name, that the first syllable would more correctly be spelt with a *p* than a *b*, this "dap" being the old perfect of "to dip," so that the name is no idle unmeaning thing, but brings out the most salient characteristic of the bird which bears it, it swift diving and "dipping" under the water at every apprehension of danger: just as in Latin a certain water-fowl is called "mergus," from "mergo."

Or taking them into the corn-fields, you may point out how the "cockle" which springs up only too luxuriantly in some of our Hampshire furrows, acquires its name from that which often it effectually does, namely from its "choking" or strangling the good seed. And the word "field" itself is worth taking note of, for it throws us back upon a period when England was covered, as is a great part of America now, with forests; "field" meaning properly a clearing where the trees have been "felled," or cut down, as in all our early English writers it is spelt without the *i*, "feld" and not "field," even as you will find in them that "wood" and "feld" are continually set over, and contrasted with, one another.

In such ways you may often improve, and without turning play-time into lesson-time, the hours of relaxation and amusement. But I must not here let escape me these words, "relaxation" and "amusement," on which I have lighted as by chance. "Amusement," or as with another striking image we call it, "recreation," what is it, and what does it affirm of itself? Why plainly this, that it must be first earned; for let us only question the word a little closer, and see what it involves. It is plainly, "à musis," that is, a temporary suspension of, and turning away from, severer studies, which severer studies are represented here by the Muses, who, I may just remind you, were the patronesses in old time not of poetry alone, but of history, geometry, and all other studies as well. What shall we then say of them, who would fain have their lives to be *all* "amusement," or who claim it otherwise than as this temporary withdrawal "à musis"? The very word condemns them; even as that other word "relaxation" does the same. How can the bow be relaxed or slackened, for this of course is the image, which has not ever been bent, whose string has never been drawn tight? Let us draw it tight by earnest toil, and then we may look to have it from time to time relaxed. Having been attentive and assiduous, then, but not otherwise, we may claim relaxation and amusement. But "attentive" and "assiduous," are themselves words which it is worth our while to realize what they mean. He then is "assiduous," who sits close to his work; he is "attentive," who stretches out his neck that so he may bring the organ of hearing nearer to the speaker, and lose none of his words. And then what a lesson the word "diligence" contains. How profitable is it for every one of us to be reminded, as we are reminded when we make ourselves aware of its derivation from "diligo," to love, that the only secret of true industry in our work is love of that work. And as there is a great truth wrapped up in "diligence," what a lie on the other hand lurks at the root of our present use of the word "indolence." This is from "in" and "doleo," not to grieve; and "indolence" is thus a state in which we have no grief or pain; so that the word, employed as we now employ it, seems to affirm that indulgence in sloth and ease is that which would constitute for us the absence of all pain. Now it may be quite true that "pain" and "pains" are often nearly allied; no one would wish to deny this; but yet these pains hand us over to true pleasures; while indolence is so far from yielding what it is so forward to promise, and we with our slothful self-indulgent hearts are so ready to expect, that Cowper spoke only truth, when, perhaps purposing expressly to witness against the falsehood of this word, he spoke of

"Lives spent in *indolence*, and therefore *sad*."

not "therefore *glad*," as the word would promise.

Let me mention another method in which these studies which I have been urging upon you, may be turned to account in your future work. Doubtless you will ever seek to cherish in your scholars, to keep lively in yourselves, that spirit and temper which attach a special value and interest to all having to do with the land of our birth, that land which the providence of God has assigned as the sphere of our life's work and of theirs. Our schools are called "national," and if we would have them such more than in name we must neglect nothing that will assist us in fostering a national spirit in them. I know not whether this is sufficiently considered among us, and yet I am sure that we can not have church schools worthy the name, and least of all in England, unless they are truly national as well. It is the anti-national character of the Romish system, though I do not in the least separate this from its anti-scriptural, but rather regard the two as most intimately cohering with one another, which mainly revolts Englishmen; as we have lately very plainly seen; and if their sense of this should ever grow weak, their protest against that system would soon lose nearly all of its energy and strength. Now here, as everywhere else, knowledge must be the food of love. Your pupils must know something about England, if they are to love it; they must see some connection of its past with its present, of what it has been with what it now is, if they are to feel that past as anything to them.

And as no impresses of the past upon the present are so abiding, so none, when once attention has been awakened to them, are so self-evident as those which names preserve; although, without this calling of the attention to them, the most broad and obvious of these foot-prints of time may very probably continue to escape our observation to the end of our lives. Leibnitz tell us, and one can quite understand, the delight with which a great German emperor, Maximilian the First, discovered that "Habsburg," the ancestral name of his house, really had a meaning, one moreover full of vigor and poetry. This he did, when he heard it by accident on the lips of a Swiss peasant, no longer cut short and thus disguised, but in its original fullness, "Habichtsburg," or "Hawk's tower," being no doubt the name of the castle which was the cradle of his race. Of all the thousands of Englishmen who are aware that the Angles and Saxons established themselves in this island, and that we are in the main descended from them, it would be curious to know how many have realized that this "England" means "Angle-land," or that in the names Essex, Sussex, and Middlesex, we preserve a record to this day of East-Saxons, South-Saxons, and Middle-Saxons, who occupied those several portions of the land; or that Norfolk and Suffolk are two broad divisions of "northern" and "southern folk," into which the East-Anglian kingdom was divided. I can not but believe that these Angles and these

Saxons, about whom our pupils may be reading, will be to them more like actual men of flesh and blood, who indeed trod this same soil which we are treading now, when we can thus point to the traces of them surviving to the present day, which they have left behind them, and which England, as long as it is England, will retain.

And then as regards the Danes — all of us who are at all acquainted with the early history of our land, will be aware how much Danish blood there is in the veins of Englishmen; what large colonies from Scandinavia (for probably as many came from Norway as from modern Denmark), settled in some parts of this island. It will be interesting to show that the limits of this Danish settlement and occupation may even now be confidently traced by the frequent occurrence in all such districts of the names of towns and villages ending in "bye," which word signified in their language, "town," as Netherby, Appleby, Derby. Thus if you examine closely a map of Lincolnshire, one of the chief seats, as is well known, of Danish immigration, you will find that well-nigh a fourth part of the towns and villages have this ending; the whole coast is indeed studded with them; while here in Hampshire it is utterly unknown.

Who that has seen London from one of its bridges, with that wondrous forest of masts stretching down the river, or that has only heard of its commerce, but would learn with interest that "London," according to the most probable etymology, is a name formed out of two Celtic words, and means, "city of ships"? Such a prophecy of the future greatness of the great commercial capital of England and of the world lay from the very first in the name which it bore; not to say that this name indicates that from earliest times, before a Roman had set his foot upon the soil, the wonderfully advantageous position of London for commerce had been discovered and improved.

You are yourselves learning, or hereafter you may be teaching others, the names and number of the English counties or shires. What a dull routine task for them and for you this may be, tasking the memory, but supplying no food for the intellect, no points of attachment for any of its higher powers to take hold of. And yet in these two little words "shire" and "county," if you would make them render up even a small part of their treasure, what lessons of English history are contained. One who knows the origin of these names, and how we come to possess such a double nomenclature, looks far into the social condition of England in that period when the rudimental germs of all that has since made it glorious and great were being laid, and by these words may show how the present links itself with the remotest past; how of a land as of a person, it may be truly said, "the child is father of the man." "Shire," as I observed just now,* is connected with "shear," "share," and is properly

* See page 203.

a portion "sheared" or "shorn" off. When a Saxon king would create an earl, it did not lie in men's thoughts, accustomed as they then were to deal with realities, that such could be, as now it may, a merely titular creation, or could exist without territorial jurisdiction; and a "share" or "shire" was assigned him to govern, which also gave him his title. But at the Conquest this Saxon officer was displaced by a Norman, the "earl" by the "count"—this title of "count," borrowed from the later Roman empire, meaning originally "companion" (comes), one who had the honor of being closest companion to his leader; and the "shire" was now the "county" (comitatus), as governed by this "comes." In that singular and inexplicable fortune of words, which causes some to disappear and die out under circumstances most favorable for life, others to hold their ground when all seemed against them, "count" has disappeared from the titles of English nobility, while "earl" has recovered its place; although in evidence of the essential identity of the two titles, or offices rather, the wife of the earl is entitled a "countess;" and in further memorial of these great changes that so long ago came over our land, the two names "shire" and "county" equally survive as household and in the main interchangeable words in our mouths.

Let us a little consider, in conclusion, how we may usefully bring our etymologies and our other notices of words to bear on the religious teaching which we would impart in our schools. To do this with much profit we must often deal with words as the queen does with the gold and silver coin of the realm, When this has been current long, and by much use and often passing from man to man, with perhaps occasional clipping in dishonest hands, has quite lost the clear brightness, the well-defined sharpness of outline, and a good part of the weight and intrinsic value which it had when first issued from the royal mint, it is the sovereign's prerogative to recall it, and issue it anew, with her image stamped on it afresh, bright, and sharp, weighty and full as at first. Now to a process such as this the true mint-masters of language will often submit the words which they use; and something of this kind we all of us may do. Where use and custom have worn away the significance of words, we too may recall and issue them afresh. And this has been the case with how many; for example, with a word which will be often in your mouths—the "lessons" of the day. What is "lessons" here for most of us but a lazy synonym for the morning and evening chapters appointed to be read in church? But realize the word "lessons," and what the church intended in calling these chapters by this name; namely, that they are to be the daily instruction of her children. Listen to them as such; address yourselves to their explanation in the spirit of this word; make your pupils regard them in this light; show them that, using this name in regard of them, they affirm them to be such, to be not in word only but in truth daily "lessons" for every one.

The "Bible" itself—with no irreverent use of the word, it may yet be no more to us than the sign by which we designate the written word of God. But if we ask ourselves what the word means, and know that it means simply "the book," so that there was a time when "bible" in English would be applied to any book (in Chaucer it is so), then how much matter of thought and reflection is here, and in this our present restriction of the word to one book, to the exclusion of all others. So prevailing, that is, has been the sense of Holy Scripture being *the* Book, the worthiest and best, that one which explained all other books, standing up in their midst —like Joseph's kingly sheaf, to which all the other sheaves did obeisance—that this name of "bible" or "book" has come to be restricted to it alone: just as "scripture" means no more than "writing;" but this inspired writing has been felt to be so far above all other writings, that this name also it has challenged as exclusively its own.

You will present, I think, to your pupils the collects which they learn from Sunday to Sunday under a more interesting aspect, when you have taught them that they probably are so called because they "collect," as into a focus, the teaching of the epistle and gospel, gathering them up in a single petition; and from this you may profitably exercise them in tracing the bond of relation which thus will be found ever to exist between the collect, and the epistle and gospel which follow it. Who again will not be pleased to know that "Whit"-Sunday is "White" Sunday, in all likelihood so called because of the multitude of "white"-robed catechumens that used upon this day of the pentecostal gifts to be presented at the font? And I am sure there is much to be learned from knowing that the "surname," as distinguished from the Christian name, is the name over and above, not the "sire"-name, or name received from the father, but "sur"-name (super nomen)—that, while there never was a time when every baptized man had not a Christian name, inasmuch as his personality before God was recognised, yet the surname, the name expressing a man's relation, not to the kingdom of God, but to the worldly society in which he lives, is only of a much later growth, an addition to the other, as the word itself declares. And what a lesson at once in the upgrowth of human society, and in the contrast between it and the heavenly society, might be appended to this explanation. There was a period when only a few had surnames, only a few, that is, had any significance or importance in the order of things temporal; while the Christian name from the first was common to every man. Surely this may be brought usefully to bear on your exposition of the first words in the Catechism.

And then, further, in regard of the long Latin words, which, with all our desire to use all plainness of speech, we yet can not do without, nor find their adequate substitutes in the other parts of our language, but which must remain the vehicles of so much of the truth by which we live — in explaining these, make it, I would say, your rule always to start, where you can, from the derivation, and to return to that as often as you can. Thus you have before you the word "revelation." How great a matter, if you can attach some distinct image to the word, and one to which your scholars, as often as they hear the word, may mentally recur. Nor is this impossible. God's revelation of himself is the drawing back of the veil or curtain which concealed him from men; not man finding out God, but God declaring or discovering himself to man; all which lies plainly in the word. Or you have the word "absolution:" many will know that it has something to do with the pardon of sins; but in how much more lively a way, to say the least, will they know this, when they know that "to absolve" means "to loosen from:" God's "absolution" of men is his releasing of them from the bands of sin with which they were tied and bound. Here every one will connect a distinct image with the word, one that will always come to his help when he would realize what its actual meaning is. That which was done for Lazarus naturally, the Lord saying in regard of him, "Loose him, and let him go," the same is done spiritually for us, when we receive the "absolution" of our sins.

Many words more suggest themselves;* but only one more I will bring forward; and that one because we shall find in it a lesson more for ourselves than for others, and it is with such a one I would fain bring these lectures to a close. How important, I would observe then, is the truth which we express

* Several of the following I had marked down, while sketching out these lectures, with the intention of using them therein; but from lack of space, or from one cause or another, have not employed them. They contain, I believe, every one of them, in their derivation or their use, or in both, something that will make it worth your pains to acquaint yourselves with them; either some fact of history, some custom of past times, some truth of the moral or spiritual world, some lively and impressive image, or other noticeable circumstance about them. In most cases Richardson's dictionary, the only one from which I can promise you effectual help, for it is the only English one in which etymology assumes the dignity of a science, will put you in the right position for judging why the word has been suggested to you. The words, to which many as good, some no doubt still better, might easily be added, are these: absurd, affable, anthem, barbarous, belief, caricature, civility, civilization, clerk, constable, courtesy, danger, delirium, devotion, dispute, enthusiasm, fanatic, feudal, fortnight, gazette, generous, genius, gentleman, gossip, habit, heresy, history, homage, husbandry, hypocrite, iniquity, integrity, intoxication, knight, legend, maxim, mercy, misunderstanding, mountebank, naughtiness, novel, obligation, peers, physician, politics, precarious, prerogative, prodigy, profane, prose, rebellion, recreant, refinement, reflection, religion, reprobate, reputation, right, romance, salary, sarcasm, sedition, sincere, sophistry, speculation, stationer, superstition, sycophant, transgression, university, urbane, verse, villany, wassail, worship.

in the naming of our work in this world our "vocation," or, which is the same finding utterance in homelier Anglo-Saxon, our "calling." What a calming, elevating, solemnizing view of the tasks which we find ourselves set in this world to do, this word would give us, if we did but realize it to the full. We did not come to our work by accident; we did not choose it for ourselves; but, under much which may wear the appearance of accident and self-choosing, came to it by God's leading and appointment. What a help is this thought to enable us to appreciate justly the dignity of our work, though it were far humbler work, even in eyes of men, than that of any one of us present! What an assistance in calming unsettled thoughts and desires, such as would make us wish to be something else than that which we are! What a source of confidence, when we are tempted to lose heart, and to doubt whether we shall be able to carry through our work with any blessing or profit to ourselves or to others! It is our "vocation," our "calling;" and He who "called" us to it, will fit us for it, and strengthen us in it.

INDEX OF WORDS.

THE END.

PHILOSOPHERS AND ACTRESSES.

By Arsene Houssaye. With beautifully-engraved Portraits of Voltaire and Madame Parabère. 2 vols. 12mo: price $2.50.

"We have here the most charming book we have read these many days,—so powerful in its fascination that we have been held for hours from our imperious labors, or needful slumbers, by the entrancing influence of its pages. One of the most desirable fruits of the prolific fields of literature of the present season."—*Portland Eclectic.*

"Two brilliant and fascinating—we had almost said, bewitching—volumes, combining information and amusement, the lightest gossip, with solid and serviceable wisdom."—*Yankee Blade.*

"It is a most admirable book, full of originality, wit, information, and philosophy. Indeed, the vividness of the book is extraordinary. The scenes and descriptions are absolutely life-like."—*Southern Literary Gazette.*

"The works of the present writer are the only ones the spirit of whose rhetoric does justice to those times, and the fascination of description and style equal the fascinations they descant upon."—*New Orleans Commercial Bulletin.*

"The author is a brilliant writer, and serves up his sketches in a sparkling manner." *Christian Freeman.*

ANCIENT EGYPT UNDER THE PHARAOHS.

By John Kendrick, M. A. In 2 vols., 12mo, price $2.50.

"No work has heretofore appeared suited to the wants of the historical student, which combined the labors of artists, travellers, interpreters and critics, during the periods from the earliest records of the monarchy to its final absorption in the empire of Alexander. This work supplies this deficiency."—*Olive Branch.*

"Not only the geography and political history of Egypt under the Pharaohs are given, but we are furnished with a minute account of the domestic manners and customs of the inhabitants, their language, laws, science, religion, agriculture, navigation and commerce."—*Commercial Advertiser.*

"These volumes present a comprehensive view of the results of the combined labors of travellers, artists, and scientific explorers, which have effected so much during the present century toward the development of Egyptian archæology and history."—*Journal of Commerce.*

"The descriptions are very vivid and one wanders, delighted with the author, through the land of Egypt, gathering at every step, new phases of her wondrous history, and ends with a more intelligent knowledge than he ever before had, of the land of the Pharaohs."—*American Spectator.*

COMPARATIVE PHYSIOGNOMY;

Or Resemblances between Men and Animals. By J. W. Redfield, M. D. In one vol., 8vo, with several hundred illustrations. price, $2.00.

"Dr. Redfield has produced a very curious, amusing, and instructive book, curious in its originality and illustrations, amusing in the comparisons and analyses, and instructive because it contains very much useful information on a too much neglected subject. It will be eagerly read and quickly appreciated."—*National Ægis.*

"The whole work exhibits a good deal of scientific research, intelligent observation, and ingenuity."—*Daily Union.*

"Highly entertaining even to those who have little time to study the science."—*Detroit Daily Advertiser.*

"This is a remarkable volume and will be read by two classes, those who study for information, and those who read for amusement. For its originality and entertaining character, we commend it to our readers."—*Albany Express.*

"It is overflowing with wit, humor, and originality, and profusely illustrated. The whole work is distinguished by vast research and knowledge."—*Knickerbocker.*

"The plan is a novel one; the proofs **striking**, and must challenge the attention of **the** curious."—*Daily Advertiser*

NOTES AND EMENDATIONS OF SHAKESPEARE.

Notes and Emendations to the Text of Shakespeare's Plays, from the Early Manuscript Corrections in a copy of the folio of 1632, in the possession of JOHN PAYNE COLLIER, Esq., F.S.A. Third edition with a fac-simile of the Manuscript Corrections. 1 vol., 12mo, cloth, $1.50.

"It is not for a moment to be doubted, we think, that in this volume a contribution has been made to the clearness and accuracy of Shakespeare's text, by far the most important of any offered or attempted since Shakespeare lived and wrote."—*Lond. Exam.*

"The corrections which Mr. Collier has here given to the world are, we venture to think, of more value than the labors of nearly all the critics on Shakespeare's text put together."—*London Literary Gazette.*

"It is a rare gem in the history of literature, and can not fail to command the attention of all the amateurs of the writings of the immortal dramatic poet."—*Ch'ston Cour.*

"It is a book absolutely indispensable to every admirer of Shakespeare who wishes to read him understandingly."—*Louisville Courier.*

"It is clear from internal evidence, that for the most part they are genuine restorations of the original plays. They carry conviction with them."—*Home Journal.*

"This volume is an almost indispensable companion to any of the editions of Shakespeare, so numerous and often important are many of the corrections."—*Register, Philadelphia.*

THE HISTORY OF THE CRUSADES.

By JOSEPH FRANÇOIS MICHAUD. Translated by W. Robson, 3 vols. 12mo., maps, $3 75.

"It is comprehensive and accurate in the detail of facts, methodical and lucid in arrangement, with a lively and flowing narrative."—*Journal of Commerce.*

"We need not say that the work of Michaud has superseded all other histories of the Crusades. This history has long been the standard work with all who could read it in its original language. Another work on the same subject is as improbable as a new history of the 'Decline and Fall of the Roman Empire.'"—*Salem Freeman.*

"The most faithful and masterly history ever written of the wild wars for the Holy Land."—*Philadelphia American Courier.*

"The ability, diligence, and faithfulness, with which Michaud has executed his great task, are undisputed; and it is to his well-filled volumes that the historical student must now resort for copious and authentic facts, and luminous views respecting this most romantic and wonderful period in the annals of the Old World."—*Boston Daily Courier.*

MARMADUKE WYVIL.

An Historical Romance of 1651, by HENRY W. HERBERT, author of the "Cavaliers of England," &c., &c. Fourteenth Edition. Revised and Corrected.

"This is one of the best works of the kind we have ever read—full of thrilling incidents and adventures in the stirring times of Cromwell, and in that style which has made the works of Mr. Herbert so popular."—*Christian Freeman, Boston.*

"The work is distinguished by the same historical knowledge, thrilling incident, and pictorial beauty of style, which have characterized all Mr. Herbert's fictions and imparted to them such a bewitching interest."—*Yankee Blade.*

"The author out of a simple plot and very few characters, has constructed a novel of deep interest and of considerable historical value. It will be found well worth reading"—*National Ægis, Worcester.*

DISCOVERY AND EXPLORATION

Of the Mississippi Valley. With the Original Narratives of Marquette, Allouez, Membré, Hennepin, and Anastase Douay. By JOHN GILMARY SHEA. With a fac-simile of the Original Map of Marquette. 1 vol., 8vo,; Cloth. Antique. $2.00.

"A volume of great and curious interest to all concerned to know the early history of this great Western land."—*Cincinnati Christian Herald.*

"We believe that this is altogether the most thorough work that has appeared on the subject to which it relates. It is the result of long-continued and diligent research, and no legitimate source of information has been left unexplored. The work combines the interest of romance with the authenticity of history."—*Puritan Recorder.*

"Mr. Shea has rendered a service to the cause of historical literature worthy of all praise by the excellent manner in which he has prepared this important publication for the press."—*Boston Traveller.*

NEWMAN'S REGAL ROME.

An Introduction to Roman History. By FRANCIS W. NEWMAN, Professor of Latin in the University College, London. 12mo, Cloth. 63 cents.

"The book, though small in compass, is evidently the work of great research and reflection, and is a valuable acquisition to historical literature."—*Courier and Enquirer.*

"A work of great erudition and power, vividly reproducing the wonderful era of Roman history under the kings. We greet it as a work of profound scholarship, genial art, and eminent interest—a work that will attract the scholar and please the general reader."—*N. Y. Evangelist.*

"Nearly all the histories in the schools should be banished, and such as this should take their places."—*Boston Journal.*

"Professor Newman's work will be found full of interest, from the light it throws on the formation of the language, the races, and the history, of ancient Rome."—*Wall-street Journal.*

THE CHEVALIERS OF FRANCE,

From the Crusaders to the Mareschals of Louis XIV. By HENRY W. HERBERT, author of "The Cavaliers of England," "Cromwell," "The Brothers," &c., &c. 1 vol. 12mo. $1.25.

"Mr. Herbert is one of the best writers of historical tales and legends in this or any other country."—*Christian Freeman.*

"This is a work of great power of thought and vividness of picturing. It is a moving panorama of the inner life of the French empire in the days of chivalry."—*Albany Spec*

"The series of works by this author, illustrative of the romance of history, is deservedly popular. They serve, indeed, to impart and impress on the mind a great deal of valuable information; for the facts of history are impartially exhibited, and the fiction presents a vivid picture of the manners and sentiments of the times."—*Journal of Commerce.*

"The work contains four historical tales or novelettes, marked by that vigor of style and beauty of description which have found so many admirers among the readers of the author's numerous romanaes."—*Lowell Journal.*

www.ingramcontent.com/pod-product-compliance
Lightning Source LLC
LaVergne TN
LVHW050519100826
845148LV00002B/383

* 9 7 8 1 4 2 5 5 2 0 6 8 7 *